For Americans—Union or Confederate—the Civil War years proved to be the most challenging time of their lives.

FOR HOME AND COUNTRY

A CIVIL WAR SCRAPBOOK

Norman Bolotin and Angela Herb

LODESTAR BOOKS
Dutton   New York

Library of Congress Cataloging-in-Publication Data

Bolotin, Norman, 1951–
   For home and country: a Civil War scrapbook / by Norman Bolotin and Angela Herb.—1st ed.
      p.   cm.—(Young readers' history of the Civil War)
   "6th book in unnumbered series"—CIP info.
   Includes bibliographical references.
   ISBN 0-525-67495-0
   1. United States—History—Civil War, 1861–1865—Pictorial works—Juvenile literature.   2. United States—History—Civil War, 1861–1865—Juvenile literature.   [1. United States—History—Civil War, 1861–1865.]
   I. Herb, Angela M.   II. Title.   III. Series.
E468.7.B65   1995
973.7'022'2—dc20   95-7896
                                                                          CIP
                                                                          AC

Published in the United States by Lodestar Books,
an affiliate of Dutton Children's Books,
a division of Penguin Books USA Inc.
375 Hudson Street
New York, New York 10014

Published simultaneously in Canada by
McClelland & Stewart, Toronto

Series development/book production: Laing Communications Inc.,
   Redmond, Washington.
Editorial management: Christine Laing
Design: Sandra Harner

Printed in the U.S.A.   First Edition   10 9 8 7 6 5 4 3 2 1

CONTENTS

ACKNOWLEDGMENTS

Several individuals provided important assistance in the creation of this book and preceding titles in the Young Readers' History of the Civil War series.

Kean Wilcox, historian and photography professor, wrote the section "Photographing the War" and furnished numerous photos from his personal collection for this and previous books.

Andrea Mark, Chicago Public Library archivist, graciously contributed her time and expertise to help us identify and obtain materials.

Erik Stuhaug, with patience and a masterful eye, created expert studio photographs for this book and hand-tinted prints for *Reconstruction: America After the Civil War*.

John and Troy Leib, of Leib Image Archives, offered research assistance and numerous historical prints, often sending the perfect photo at a moment's notice.

Thomas J. McCarthy provided access to his extensive collection of vintage Civil War books, documents, and ephemera, and was a source of quick information on myriad Civil War details.

Brian C. Pohanka, who wrote the sections "War Fever" and "Citizen to Soldier," is one of the foremost Civil War historians in the United States. His critical eye and wealth of knowledge have been integral to the success of our entire series.

From the moment we proposed the series, two individuals at Dutton/Lodestar Books have been greatly supportive. Christopher Franceschelli, President and Publisher of Dutton Children's Books, had the foresight to recognize that there was a need for such illustrated, readable history books for children. Virginia Buckley, Lodestar Editorial Director, provided a keen and challenging editorial eye that kept us on our toes, while allowing us a level of creative control infrequently seen in the publishing industry.

Christine Laing, editorial director for the series, ensured that young readers throughout the country received books that are fun to read *and* academically sound. Sandra Harner, art director/designer for all six books, once again proved to be professional, patient, and a wonderful talent.

Finally, Angela Herb, coauthor of this book, should have received top billing for her hard work and deserves special recognition for tact and wisdom beyond her years.

Norman Bolotin
President, Laing Communications

to Sánchez, Schwarzbach,
and Kilgore

—AH

FOUR LONG YEARS

Abraham Lincoln

"*We, the people of the State of South Carolina, in Convention assembled, do declare and ordain . . . that the union now subsisting between South Carolina and other States under the name of the United States of America is hereby dissolved.*"

South Carolina's ordinance to secede

Jefferson Davis

1860

1861

November 6, 1860
Abraham Lincoln is elected sixteenth president of the United States—a country bitterly divided over the issues of slavery and states' rights. The increasingly different lifestyles and economies of the North and South make it difficult for the states to compromise.

December 20, 1860
After years of fierce political quarrels, South Carolina secedes from the Union. It is soon followed by ten more states: Mississippi, Florida, Alabama, Georgia, Louisiana, Texas, Virginia, Arkansas, Tennessee, and North Carolina. Together, they form a new country: the Confederate States of America. President Lincoln refuses to recognize the Confederate States as a separate country, declaring that states do not have the right to leave the Union.

February 9, 1861
Jefferson Davis, a former U.S. senator from Mississippi, is elected president of the Confederacy. Tensions between the North and South continue to swell.

April 12, 1861
The war begins! Union troops at Fort Sumter, in Charleston harbor, South Carolina, refuse to evacuate the fort and are bombarded by Confederate troops. No lives are lost in this first battle of the war. During the weeks that follow, thousands of men rush to volunteer as soldiers.

July 21, 1861
The Confederates soundly defeat the Union in the first major battle of the war, the Battle of Bull Run at Manassas, Virginia. Three thousand Union soldiers and 2,000 Confederates are dead, wounded, or missing. Seeing the bloody results of the battle, Americans begin to lose their romantic view of war.

Fort Sumter

After the Battle of Antietam

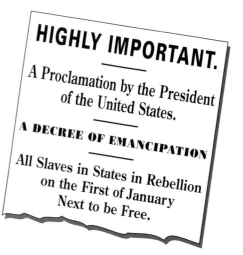

HIGHLY IMPORTANT.

A Proclamation by the President of the United States.

A DECREE OF EMANCIPATION

All Slaves in States in Rebellion on the First of January Next to be Free.

1862

February 15, 1862
After three days of fighting, Union General Ulysses S. Grant (who later becomes the eighteenth president of the United States) captures Fort Donelson, Tennessee, on the Cumberland River—the first major loss for the Confederacy.

April 6, 1862
Confederate troops surprise Union soldiers in an early morning attack, at the Battle of Shiloh, Tennessee. In two days of heavy fighting, the Confederates crush Union troops. To that date, the Battle of Shiloh is the largest battle ever fought in America: 13,000 casualties for the North, and 11,700 for the South.

April 16, 1862
With the number of volunteers dwindling, the Confederate Congress enacts the first conscription law in American history. The government's decision to draft soldiers is highly unpopular with most Southerners.

June 25–July 1, 1862
Union General George McClellan's army has advanced to within seven miles of the Confederate capital of Richmond, Virginia. During a week-long series of battles, known as the Seven Days' campaign, Confederate General Robert E. Lee's men force the Union troops back twenty-three miles. Northern morale plummets, and both sides suffer severe losses: the Confederacy, 20,000 men; the Union, almost 16,000.

August 28–30, 1862
General Lee's troops are victorious again: The Union is soundly defeated at Manassas, Virginia, in the second Battle of Bull Run.

September 17, 1862
With nearly 23,000 soldiers killed, wounded, or missing, the Battle of Antietam, Maryland, is the single bloodiest day of the war. General McClellan's army succeeds in preventing General Lee from invading the North.

September 22, 1862
Lincoln issues the Emancipation Proclamation, officially declaring the end of slavery in the South. Many blacks flee north, hoping for new opportunities and a chance to fight for the Union.

December 11–13, 1862
Union General Ambrose Burnside's troops cross the Rappahannock River on pontoon bridges and take the Confederate city of Fredericksburg, Virginia. Attempting to move on to Richmond, Burnside makes a series of mistakes, which result in a horrible defeat for the North and 12,600 Union casualties.

December 31, 1862–January 2, 1863
At the Battle of Murfreesboro/Stones River, Tennessee, both armies suffer 13,000 casualties, with the Union winning by a narrow margin. The great loss of men weakens the South (with its smaller population) more than the North.

Robert E. Lee

Ulysses S. Grant

VICKSBURG.

VICTORY!

Gen. Grant's Celebration of the Fourth of July.

Unconditional Surrender of the Rebel Stronghold.

1863

March 3, 1863
The U.S. Congress enacts the Enrollment Act of 1863. The draft law induces more men to volunteer but creates widespread corruption in the enlistment process.

May 1–3, 1863
At the Battle of Chancellorsville, Virginia, the Confederacy is victorious but suffers many casualties, including one of its best military leaders. In the shadowy night, Confederate General Thomas "Stonewall" Jackson is mistakenly shot by his own men. He dies eight days later.

July 1–3, 1863
The Battle of Gettysburg, Pennsylvania, is a turning point in the war. After a series of victories in Virginia, General Lee's Confederate troops aim to win a battle on northern soil but are defeated by Union troops under the command of General George Meade. Although the war continues for two more years, the Confederacy never regains the momentum of its early victories.

July 4, 1863
Vicksburg, Mississippi, under siege since May 18, surrenders to General Grant, giving the Union control of the Mississippi River.

September 18–20, 1863
With heavy losses on both sides (more than 34,000 total casualties), the Confederacy wins the Battle of Chickamauga, Georgia, but gains little strategic advantage.

May 5–6, 1864
In a thickly wooded landscape in northern Virginia, General Grant refuses to retreat despite high casualties. The result is a much-needed boost to Union morale against General Lee at the Battle of the Wilderness.

May 8–19, 1864
The fighting in northern Virginia continues at Spotsylvania. In a series of fierce engagements, some of the worst fighting occurs on May 12 at the "Bloody Angle," a several-hundred-yard-long area of trenches where soldiers battle hand to hand in the rain for eighteen hours.

A Confederate casualty

General Lee surrenders

AWFUL EVENT.
President Lincoln Shot by an Assassin.
The Deed Done at Ford's Theatre Last Night.
THE ACT OF A DESPERATE REBEL
The President Still Alive at Last Accounts.
No Hopes Entertained of His Recovery.

Andrew Johnson

1864

September 2, 1864
Union General William Tecumseh Sherman captures Atlanta, Georgia.

November 8, 1864
Abraham Lincoln is reelected president of the United States.

June 3, 1864
At dawn on June 3, 1864, less than a year before the end of the war, General Grant's army unsuccessfully attacks General Lee's troops at the Battle of Cold Harbor, Virginia. In just twenty minutes, 7,000 Union men fall dead or wounded.

November 16, 1864
General Sherman leaves Atlanta, beginning his destructive March to the Sea. His goal is to end the war by destroying the South's land and resources.

1865

April 3, 1865
Union troops occupy Richmond and Petersburg, Virginia.

April 9, 1865
After the Battle of Appomattox, Virginia, General Lee surrenders, officially ending the war, although the last armed Confederate soldiers do not surrender until the following month.

April 15, 1865
Andrew Johnson, Lincoln's vice president, is sworn in as president.

April 14, 1865
John Wilkes Booth shoots President Lincoln at Ford's Theater in Washington, D.C. Lincoln dies the following day.

May 23–24, 1865
The Union Army stages its last grand review of troops down Pennsylvania Avenue in Washington, D.C. The parade lasts for two days, after which the soldiers are mustered out to return home.

August 2, 1865
Confederate sailors on the CSS Shenandoah, stationed in the Bering Sea, are the last to receive news that the war has ended. On November 6, they surrender in Liverpool, England.

The Grand Review in Washington, D.C.

*"**I** was awakened about half past four this morning by the booming of a cannon, and it has been going on steadily ever since—the firing is constant and rapid—with what results we don't yet know."*

Mrs. Louis Trezevant Wigfall,
resident of Charleston, in a letter to
her daughter Louise, April 12, 1861

Introduction

WAR FEVER

THOMAS SOUTHWICK stood at the corner of Ann Street and Broadway and marveled at the change that had come over his city. "THE WAR COMMENCED!" "FORT SUMTER FALLEN!" "THE UNION FOREVER!" The headlines jumped off the pages of the New York papers, echoed by dozens of newsboys who hurried through the crowded streets of Manhattan. As the shrill voices rang in his ears, Southwick knew there was no escaping the awful fact that America was at war.

Standing only an inch over five feet and weighing less than one hundred pounds, Southwick appeared much younger than his twenty-four years. As a boy, he too had sold papers to help support his brothers and sisters after their parents died. For the last few years, he had worked for the Third Avenue Railway, but that warm spring afternoon he could find little reason to go to work. Like so many other young Americans, Thomas Southwick had caught the "war fever."

Though he never had the opportunity to go to college, from his earliest childhood Southwick had loved to read. He could quote the Bible, enjoyed the exciting tales of Greek and Roman mythology, and

Opposite: The war began on April 12, 1861, when Confederate troops bombed Fort Sumter in Charleston, South Carolina. In the early morning hours, residents of the city gathered on rooftops to watch shells exploding over the harbor. Two days later, Union troops surrendered the island fort; no lives were lost in the first battle of the war.

was fond of Shakespeare, saving his hard-earned wages so he could attend performances of *Hamlet* and *Macbeth* in New York theaters. He had grown up with stories of the Revolutionary War and loved to study the military campaigns of Julius Caesar and Napoleon. "Eventually the perusal of war-like portions of history became my chief delight," Southwick said, "and sometimes caused me to sigh for an opportunity to distinguish myself."

But somehow this war did not seem right to Southwick. As the debate over slavery and states' rights had escalated, dividing the country into two antagonistic factions, he found himself sympathizing with the South. Like many New Yorkers, Southwick was a Democrat and had voted against Abraham Lincoln in the election of 1860. He had little use for the abolitionists and their crusade against slavery; even if

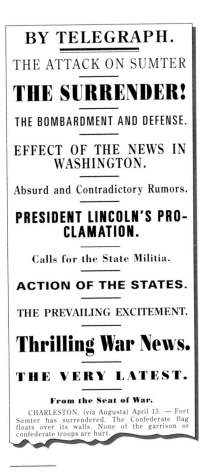

THE WAR COMMENCED.

The First Gun Fired by Fort Moultrie Against Fort Sumter.

THE BOMBARDMENT CONTINUED ALL DAY.

Spirited Return from Major Anderson's Guns.

The Firing from Fort Sumter Ceased for the Night.

Hostilities to Commence Again at Daylight.

BY TELEGRAPH.

THE ATTACK ON SUMTER

THE SURRENDER!

THE BOMBARDMENT AND DEFENSE.

EFFECT OF THE NEWS IN WASHINGTON.

Absurd and Contradictory Rumors.

PRESIDENT LINCOLN'S PRO-CLAMATION.

Calls for the State Militia.

ACTION OF THE STATES.

THE PREVAILING EXCITEMENT.

Thrilling War News.

THE VERY LATEST.

From the Seat of War.

CHARLESTON, (via Augusta) April 13. — Fort Sumter has surrendered. The Confederate flag floats over its walls. None of the garrison or confederate troops are hurt.

Lincoln was not an outright abolitionist, the president certainly seemed to lean in that direction. "The South would never submit to the election of a sectional president," Southwick believed. "They would fight for their rights under the Constitution."

And so they had. The secession of South Carolina, the firing upon Fort Sumter, the withdrawal of more southern states from the Union, and President Lincoln's call for troops to put down the rebellion—each event pushed America, and Thomas Southwick, closer to war.

The young man stood on the street corner and wrestled with his conscience. Broadway was overflowing with people, and all the buildings—P. T. Barnum's Museum, the Astor House Hotel—were covered with flags and bunting. The distant sound of fifes and drums grew louder. Cheering began as a column of troops approached, marching off to battle for their country and their cause.

When he saw the soldiers, proud, determined, and confident, Thomas Southwick's misgivings began to dissolve. "It may have been the music, or the polished bayonets flashing in the bright sunlight," he recalled. "There was something thrilling in the thought that these brave young fellows were going to battle . . . for what they believed to be right." When he caught sight of the stars and stripes, "the glorious old flag," Southwick's mind was made up. "I shouted and yelled until I was hoarse. Tears gushed into my eyes and I turned away firmly resolved to defend that flag against any that would raise their hands against it, whether they were my countrymen or not."

Having made up his mind to enlist, Southwick set about the task of finding a regiment that would live up to his boyish dreams of glory and adventure. Officers busily signed up recruits on almost every block. The men were desperate to get to the battlefield, worried the war would be over before they got a chance to fight.

Southwick didn't like the looks of some of these volunteers— they were too loud, too rough, too drunk. As a boy, he had belonged to a neighborhood gang, the "Seventeenth Streeters," and had become a pretty good boxer. But if he was going to risk his life for the noble cause of the Union, Southwick wanted to serve with gentlemen, not ruffians.

Finally, he found a unit that lived up to his expectations. The Fifth New York Volunteer Infantry had all the makings of an elite outfit. Their commander was a twenty-year veteran of the New York Militia, the officers seemed to know their business, and the regiment was going to be issued the flashy and exotic Zouave uniform: short blue jackets, baggy red trousers, and a tasseled fez, just like the French Army wore in North Africa. Surely membership

in the Zouaves promised the sort of excitement and adventure he had imagined from all of his reading.

Southwick stood in the recruiting office with a dozen other young men as a doctor passed down the line looking them over. Even though he had added an extra inch of heel to his boots, Southwick was nervous. "I was so small and insignificant looking beside my comrades that I felt quite certain of being rejected," he recalled. But he need not have worried. The doctor tapped his chest and back, asked him to raise his arms over his head, and then pronounced him

Early in the war, troops were sent off with much fanfare—bands played and crowds waved and cheered. Here, the First Michigan Volunteer Infantry receives its flags as hundreds of people gather in the streets of Detroit to bid them farewell.

VOLUNTEERS
WANTED !
FROM
WINNEBAGO COUNTY!

"We will Defend the Flag of our Fathers, and Maintain the Integrity of the Union."

Notice is Hereby Given,
That the Roll for the enlistment of Volunteers to fill up the ranks of the
ROCKFORD ZOUAVES,
To the number that the law requires, to serve at a moment's notice from the Governor, will be open from this date until filled, between the hours of 10 A. M. and 4 P. M., each day.
Rockford, April 17th, 1861.

G. NEVIUS, Capt.

fit for military service. "You are what we call a pony," the doctor said. The other volunteers smiled, and "Pony" became Thomas Southwick's nickname for the rest of his military career.

Pony Southwick rushed home, gathered a few extra shirts and socks in a bundle, tossed in his dog-eared volume of Shakespeare's plays, and bid a tearful good-bye to his family. He was off, as the

Recruits marched off to war in nervous anticipation of their first battle experience. Many referred to combat as "seeing the elephant," a phrase that developed from the practice of circuses offering free admission to boys who helped water the elephants. The danger of working with the magnificent beasts, which could crush a boy in one step, was similar to the "price" a soldier paid for seeing the exciting "show" of battle—exposing himself to flying bullets and bursting shells, and the risk of death.

slang expression of the period went, "to see the elephant"—to face both the exhilaration and danger of war.

Throughout the North and South, tens of thousands of volunteers rushed to the call, swept away by the same patriotic enthusiasm that prompted Thomas Southwick to enlist. "Excitement was a white heat," noted John W. Stevens, a Confederate recruit from Texas: "Our patriotism was just bubbling up and boiling over and frying and fizzling." As the bands played "Dixie" and "The Bonnie Blue Flag," Virginian Fannie Beers joined other loyal southern women in helping to outfit their departing loved ones with handsome new uniforms. "The Confederate gray was then a thing of beauty," she remembered, "the outer garb of true and noble souls. Every man who wore it became ennobled in the eyes of every woman."

Many Confederates refused to believe that they were fighting to preserve slavery. Robert Stiles, a law student and graduate of Yale

University, left his home in Connecticut to fight for Virginia because he felt the southern cause was just. "The great majority of them had never owned a slave," Stiles wrote of his fellow soldiers. They had taken a stand, Stiles thought, because of "the distinct threat of invasion" by Federal troops intent on trampling the rights of the individual states. Stiles and his comrades had a motto they swore to live by, and if need be, to die by: "With me is Right, before me is Duty, *behind me is Home.*"

While at first the majority of Northerners, President Lincoln included, didn't accept the abolition of slavery as a goal of the Union, some viewed the emancipation of black Americans as a sacred duty. The impassioned speeches of Wendell Phillips, William Lloyd Garrison, and Frederick Douglass had not fallen on deaf ears. Colonel James C. Rice of the Forty-fourth New York Regiment told his soldiers, "I believe that it is God's divine purpose, having used the wrath of the South to commence this war, to cause that wrath to praise Him by the freedom of every slave." While this view was unpopular in 1861, by 1863, freedom for slaves had become a focal point of Lincoln's philosophy and of the Union cause.

America was at war with itself, and to Yankee and rebel alike, the causes seemed clear and the glory and excitement certain. But, as the war raged on for four years, the bloody consequences of the conflict took the nation by surprise. For the thousands of soldiers so far from home, and the civilians who stood by as their towns and cities were bombarded, the focus turned to courage and survival. ☆

CITIZEN TO SOLDIER

Like many volunteers, these three young men from Rhode Island were probably as excited to have their portrait taken as they were to enlist. Rather than wait to be issued their full uniforms, they rushed to the photography studio still wearing some of their civilian clothes.

The glamour of military life faded quickly as soldiers spent long hours marching and drilling in companies of one hundred men. After the soldiers mastered these maneuvers, companies were combined to train as larger regiments and brigades.

*"**I** must record here that I little dreamed of the wild life in which I was so soon to take an active part. I was totally ignorant of military matters. Did not know the color of a United States uniform—never had seen a United States soldier—hardly knew the colors of the Stars and Stripes. . . . I was a . . . country youth that had never been scarcely a Dozen miles from his mother's door steps."*

W. H. H. Barker, volunteer from Iowa

Early in the war, many northern states, including Massachusetts, Pennsylvania, New York, and New Hampshire, dressed their soldiers in gray uniforms. This Union volunteer is wearing full marching equipment, though he probably added the bowie knife and pistol in his belt just for this portrait.

W<small>HATEVER THEIR</small> motivation for taking up arms, Yankees and rebels alike had to make the transition from citizen to soldier. It was not as simple as putting on a snappy uniform, strapping on a knapsack, and shouldering a musket. Only through the acceptance of strict and often arbitrary discipline could the eager volunteers hope to master their duty. "It takes a raw recruit some time to learn that he is not to think or suggest, but obey," Union volunteer Warren Lee Goss discovered. "I acquired it at last, in humility and mud, but it was tough."

Although advances in technology had made weapons more deadly than ever before, the military tactics of the 1860s did not differ greatly from those used by Napoleon fifty years earlier in Europe. The army trained soldiers not to think as individuals, but to fight as a block of men following orders. The typical Civil War unit was the regiment—ten companies of one hundred men each. The regimental commander—a colonel—had to master the complex choreography of drill that would enable his company

Commanders drilled soldiers in marching, shooting, and charging—over and over again. The carefree, enthusiastic volunteers found it hard and boring work; but, as soldiers they had to be prepared to follow orders amidst the chaos of battle—with shells bursting and thousands of rifles firing.

In newspaper ads, companies tempted new recruits with the latest inventions, from pocketed belts to bullet-proof vests. However, as with the nine-and-a-half-pound stove pictured here, soldiers soon discarded all but the most necessary items.

commanders—captains—to maneuver their formations on the parade ground, and, ultimately, the battlefield.

Since the typical Civil War soldier could fire no more than three shots a minute with his muzzle-loading rifle, the drill manuals stressed firepower, rather than target practice, as the way to overcome the enemy. Troops were trained to line up elbow to elbow in tight battle lines, advance on the enemy, and blast a way through with massed volleys from their rifles. Dozens or even hundreds of men might be shot down, but the survivors were expected to close the gaps in their lines and press on, using their fearsome bayonets, if necessary, to fight their opponents hand to hand.

The only way that free-thinking individuals could be turned into fighting "machines," able to follow orders without a pause, was to drill until the drill became second nature, an automatic reflex. And for officers as new to their job as the privates in the ranks, this was not an easy task.

Writing home to his family in Pennsylvania, teenage soldier Oliver Wilcox Norton summed up a typical day in a Civil War training camp: "The first thing in the morning is drill, then drill, then drill again. Then drill, drill, a little more drill. Then drill, and lastly drill. Between drills, we drill, and sometimes stop to eat a little and have roll call."

Norton was joking, of course, but there was an element of truth to what

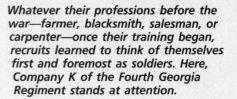

Whatever their professions before the war—farmer, blacksmith, salesman, or carpenter—once their training began, recruits learned to think of themselves first and foremost as soldiers. Here, Company K of the Fourth Georgia Regiment stands at attention.

This Confederate soldier from El Paso, Texas, was responsible for handling ordnance (ammunition), as indicated by the flaming bomb insignia on the upturned brim of his hat.

In the army, everything was done according to a system of rules, and anyone who fought the system was likely to be punished. A soldier might be forced to march back and forth wearing a knapsack filled with bricks, or to straddle a sawhorse all day in front of his fellow soldiers. For some infractions, punishments could be much more severe. The penalty for desertion, or for falling asleep on sentry duty, was death by firing squad. In this illustration, a soldier convicted of shooting his sergeant during an argument is being hanged.

he wrote: He was learning to be a soldier.

Young Alexander Hunter, who had been forced to flee his home town of Alexandria, Virginia, when it was occupied by Yankee troops in the first weeks of the war, expressed similar sentiments. "One drill was hardly over before another was called," he wrote. "It was arduous labor, harder than grubbing, stump-pulling, or cracking rocks on a turnpike."

Along with all the drilling, soldiers had to get used to following military schedules and regulations every minute of the day. When the drums and bugles sounded reveille, they had to get up no matter how tired they were. And when "lights out" or "taps" was played, they had to go quietly to their tents for the night. There were roll calls to answer, work details to perform, and guard duty to be carried out. If a soldier was sick, he waited for "sick call" to be played on the musicians' fifes and drums before he reported to the regimental surgeon for treatment.

But for most, soldiering simply meant marching—often twenty to forty miles a day, wearing a scratchy wool uniform and carrying up to fifty pounds of equipment. The first weeks in the field weeded out the physically unfit, and the men began to realize their worst enemy would not be bullets fired by the opposing side but disease and illness brought on by the hardships of camp life.

In the end, they mastered the drill, learned to accept the discipline of the army, and endured the hardships of service. At that point, they were indeed soldiers, with a soldier's pride—ready to face their trial by fire. ☆

OUTFITTING THE TROOPS

Women feverishly sewed, knitted, and weaved to help outfit the troops, although neither the recruits nor the seamstresses had a clear idea of what camp life would be like. Many soldiers headed off with gear they would never use. Here, a southern woman makes a "havelock" for a Confederate soldier; the linen headgear, invented by a British general stationed in India, was designed to shade soldiers from the glaring southern sun. Word soon got out that the men had little need for the strange-looking headpieces, and women concentrated on more practical items.

This Confederate volunteer joined an infantry company in 1861 and proudly donned a fancy uniform, with expensive piping at the collar and cuffs. His white dress gloves were appropriate for parades and ceremonies, but useless in the field.

The Confederate Army accepted men and boys of all ages as the South became desperate to fill their ranks. This older soldier strikes a ready-for-battle pose, with his revolver tucked in his belt. His bloused shirt and dark jacket were a popular style with some Southerners.

A YEAR AND A HALF after the war began, Mary Chesnut stood on a Richmond, Virginia, sidewalk and watched ten thousand Confederate soldiers march by. "We had seen nothing like this before," she thought. "Such rags and tags, nothing alike—most garments and arms had been taken from the enemy. . . . [They had] tin pans and pots tied to their waists, bread or bacon stuck on the ends of their bayonets. . . . They did not seem to know their shabby condition."

Unlike the handsomely dressed troops who marched off in 1861, by the second year of the war, most soldiers appeared rough and worn from their experiences in the field.

According to regulations, the Confederate soldier's official uniform was to consist of a long gray shirt with light blue trousers and a gray flannel overcoat. But men who enlisted expecting fancy jackets, shiny buttons, and stylish caps soon realized the government did not have enough uniforms for all its soldiers. By the middle of the war, the ragged, mismatched troops Mary Chesnut described were a common sight.

The crossed cannon insignia on this Union lieutenant's hat indicates that he was an artilleryman. Soldiers dressed in their finest clothes when they posed for a photograph, but spent most of their days dressed in scratchy wool shirts and roughly made pants.

This member of the Mount Vernon Guards, a Confederate regiment from Virginia, headed off to war in an ornately buttoned jacket.

By the middle of the war, many soldiers considered themselves lucky if they owned one full set of clothing—hopefully one with few holes in the pants, socks, and shoes.

Men often wrote to their families asking for homemade clothing, and, after battles, they scavenged garments from dead soldiers—Union or Confederate. As cloth and dye grew scarce, instead of machine-made Confederate gray cloth, some wore "butternut" material—shirts and pants made of homespun cotton and wool that was dyed brown with walnut shells.

Union soldiers fared only a bit better. Most wore a standard dark blue jacket with light blue pants, a blue cap, and heavy black shoes, which they called gunboats. Even though they had factory-made clothing, it was often difficult for Union troops to obtain adequate uniforms.

One recruit recalled that, when their uniforms were distributed, "scarcely one man in ten was fitted. Tall men had . . . short pantaloons, and . . . short men . . . received the long [ones]. One man's cap was perched away up on the top of his head, while another rested on his ears." The men slowly solved the problem: "By trading off, the large men gradually got the large garments and the little men the small, so that in a few days we were all pretty well suited."

To add to the confusion, many volunteer regiments—north and

The French-fashioned Zouave uniform was popular on both sides. With baggy pants and a sash at the waist, as well as a tasseled hat and white leggings, the outfits were considered foreign and exotic.

> *"We have had a hard time of it.... Many are barefoot as the country is rough and stony. The soles of my boots are worn off and for the past two days I have marched with my feet wound in pieces of cotton tenting. My feet are quite sore."*
>
> From a member of the First Michigan Volunteer Infantry, in a letter to his friends, April 1865

This account details Pennsylvania private Isaac Bickel's clothing as issued to him in the fall of 1864. Bickel, who could not write (he acknowledged receipt of his clothes by signing an "X"), enlisted on August 27. By September, he had his hat, shirt, pants, socks, underwear, and blankets; but he didn't receive his coat until November!

A member of
the Kentucky
Rifle Brigade

A Tennessee
Sharpshooter

south—wore uniforms of their own design. Distinctive clothing styles allowed a regiment its own identity; not only were they fighting for their country and their state but for their community and heritage as well. Financed by fund-raising drives or donations from wealthy businessmen, organized regiments wore everything from Scottish kilts to buckskin trousers.

At times, the jumble of uniforms had deadly consequences, as troops mistook fellow soldiers for the enemy and opened fire. Though the Civil War is often referred to as the fight between the "blue" and "gray," identifying a Union or Confederate soldier by the color or style of his uniform was not such a simple task. ☆

A Confederate
marine

A *"housewife"—a small sewing kit—was essential. Veteran soldiers traveled lightly, carrying few extra items; when their clothes wore out, they mended them until replacements could be found. Men who had never used a needle and thread before became experts at fixing rips, patching holes, and sewing on buttons.*

THE RIGORS OF WAR

Many battles took place on difficult terrain—hillsides covered with trees and shrubs, muddy fields, and riverbanks. Here, Union troops do their best to drag a cannon through a marsh.

Once set up in an encampment, artillerymen spent hours on guard, waiting for action. In the photo below, a Union soldier stands in a post outside Atlanta, Georgia. The Confederates could not stop General Sherman's Union Army, which captured the city in September 1864.

Women, often the wives of soldiers, washed laundry and cooked for Union troops stationed near northern cities. When settled in semi-permanent camps, some soldiers brought their families to live with them; but when the armies marched from battle to battle, few civilians followed.

*"**T**he soldier's life cannot be an easy one. . . . It is not only to bear arms, [and] to stand sentinel at night, but . . . often to unload boats, dig wells, throw up breastworks, repair railroads, clear away the forest, and build bridges. Ease is no part of his experience. Rest is out of the question."*

Reverend J. B. Rogers, chaplain, U.S. Army

Twenty-year-old Jason L. Ellis enlisted in Company I, Eighteenth Iowa Infantry Volunteers, in Des Moines on July 19, 1862. Five days later, he was sworn into service. In his diary, he wrote, "All of the girls came up to see us sworn in. We had fine times that day."

The excitement continued as Ellis and his company marched out of town: "August 11, [we] pulled up stakes and started for St. Louis; reached Davenport at sundown; such cheering from the people I never heard before; were cheered at Rock Island, also; reached Muscatine at midnight; cheering again."

But as they marched farther from home, Ellis began to realize that being a soldier was not an easy job. "August 12th, five miles below Keokuk is Alexandria, Mo.; no cheering. August 18th, hot day . . . about fifty of our men gave out. Sept. 11th, it began to rain harder than ever; overflowed our camp; water in our tents two feet deep."

Ellis didn't let the difficulties of marching put a damper on his patriotism. From near Springfield, Missouri, he wrote to his parents, "It was to help put down this Rebellion that I came into the army. I am going to do my best. . . . Ma, I hope you are gratified that you had a son that was willing to . . . sustain the good old flag."

Ellis's strong convictions helped him bear the endless work details and ever-present illnesses: "Sept. 12, set up all night with a sick soldier who had

Cavalrymen, who often worked as scouts and supply-line raiders, had to move quickly. This Union sergeant carries a light load—his blanket bedroll, food, a tin cup, and a sidearm.

You have no idea how dirty and irksome the camp life is. . . . The weather is exceedingly hot and dusty. We send three miles for water. With most . . . ablution [washing] is limited to face and hands, which rarely show the proper application of water. I write upon my knee, at present, as our table is otherwise employed.

James Chesnut, Jr.

From a letter to his wife, Mary, June 22, 1861

Union troops from the Fifth New Hampshire and Sixty-fourth New York build a bridge over the Chickahominy River as part of General McClellan's efforts to advance toward the Confederate capital of Richmond, Virginia.

During winter, some troops camped in one location for many months and the men had time to construct more than tents to fend off the cold. When possible, they chopped down trees for firewood and built log huts. Here, the soldiers have made a rough boardwalk to cover the muddy ground.

congestive chills. I got some mustard and whiskey; put on mustard plaster, and bathed him in whiskey; in the morning he was better.

Sept. 15th, at work cutting down timber and building entrenchments."

During the weeks of hard work, boredom could become an enemy in itself. Sergeant James O'Bleness, another volunteer from Iowa, faithfully recorded each day's events in his diary. In between skirmishes with the enemy, the events of one day often blended into the next.

May 1 — Commenced the fight at Port Gibson; came out victorious; lay on the field over night.

May 2 — In the morning we started out to begin again and the Rebels had run. We marched to Port Gibson and camped.

May 3 — We are now fixing to march after the Rebels.

May 4 — In camp at Port Gibson. Are ordered to be ready to march at a moment's notice.

May 5 — Marched about twelve miles and camped.

May 6 — Are camped at Willow Springs Creek; have nothing but beef and corn-meal to eat.

May 7 — Marched twelve miles and camped; had nothing to eat to-day.

May 8 — Still in camp.

May 9 — Still in camp.

May 10 — Left Rock Springs; marched ten miles and camped.

But, finally, the order to move would come, and a soldier had to be ready for anything.

Many soldiers had had little schooling and their letters and diaries contain misspellings. Still, their words convey the intense emotions and real dangers they faced.

"It was planed to march 20 miles that night. . . . We had marched quietly for . . . 10 miles—when there came on the most severe electrical storm. . . . It began with an awfull display of lightening and thunder foolowed by intense darkness and a perfect deluge of rain . . . that put the roads into a flood of wild rushing waters. . . . A real Hurrycane fell upon us . . . strewing trees and limbs on to our heads and filling the roads with debree. . . . It was impossible for any one to see his hands before his eyes. . . . Our [horses] . . . became uncontrolible and would dash against tree[s] or other obstructions injuring themselves or their riders. . . . The entire command was totally disorganized and scattered."

W. H. H. Barker

This seemingly ordinary group of men was as important to the North's success as the frontline troops. As secret service agents, their job included everything from protecting Union leaders to spying on the South.

Recruitment posters lured men into the army by promising a cash reward, comfortable quarters, and full meals.

Jason Ellis continued in his diary: "Oct. 3d, . . . ordered to march; struck tents and got ready at 9 p.m.; marched all night towards the enemy as fast as we could walk, and double-quick in part. At four in the morning we were fired into by bushwhackers. . . . up rode about one hundred Rebels within ten rods of us, and ordered us to halt. . . . Our guns were not loaded. I tried to load mine running; fell down two or three times; tore my clothes; skinned my nose; bullets whizzed past my head. . . . It was raining very hard; on we went; reached the battlefield; . . . saw the Kansas troops advancing . . . but when they saw us they ran south as fast as they could go; throwing away guns, blankets, and ammunition, burning up wagons, and destroying provisions. We went two days and nights without anything to eat but beef without salt."

Ellis was becoming a hardened veteran, though on

A Union infantryman displays his full field gear—leather knapsack, blanket bedroll, canteen, ammunition, and weapons. Sturdy leather straps held his heavy equipment in place as he marched.

This artist's drawing from a Harper's Weekly newspaper shows a long line of Union troops headed by General Sheridan marching through the Shenandoah Valley in Virginia. While northern troops far outnumbered the Confederates, few were prepared for the unbearable heat they encountered in the South.

General Grant's troops form a line of defense against charging southern soldiers who were attempting to recapture Fort Harrison, outside Richmond, in September 1864. Soldiers faced terrible odds on both sides during the war: One in ten would be wounded; one in sixty-five would die from their wounds. Even worse, one in thirteen would die from disease.

Oliver Daugherty, a member of the Eleventh Indiana Infantry known as Wallace's Zouaves, poses for a portrait on April 28, 1862, at Pittsburgh Landing, Tennessee, just after the famous Battle of Shiloh.

Behind sturdy, cannon-enforced walls, Union troops camp outside the city of Atlanta. Soldiers became accustomed to the sound of gun and artillery fire; when they weren't fighting, they went about their business—napping, eating, writing letters, or playing cards.

Dear Father,

... We got [to Fort Donelson] on St. Valentine's Day. You have heard all about the battle fought there, and it is no use for me to describe it. We had to stay out all night of the 14th without tents or blankets, and it was very cold. I suffered more that night from cold than ever before in my life. ... The usual mishaps of remaining out of provisions, etc., befell us; but we got some pilot bread and some bacon just before going into battle. ... When we received the order "Forward!" we went up the hill in a full run, the rebels dropping our boys in rows. ... I got my eye on a bunch of them, and took sight every time I shot. Sometimes I could see the man drop—thought at the time that I killed three. While I was shooting ... I received a shot in the shin ... breaking the small bone and making two holes in the calf of my leg. ... Before I was wounded I had my gun spoiled by being hit with a ball, so I had to take a fallen man's gun and use it. I was wounded about one o'clock, and it took me till nearly sundown to crawl off, and I almost froze. I was slightly wounded twice in leaving the field. Once in the head by a small piece of shell, and once on the forefinger of the right hand, splitting the knuckle. ... My wounds are not at all dangerous. I would write plainer but for the wound on my knuckle.

Yours, affectionately,
A. Slatten

Andrew Slatten, a young lawyer, answered the call to arms early in the war, enlisting in Company D, Second Iowa Regiment, in the spring of 1861. One year later, after the Battle of Fort Donelson, Tennessee, Slatten wrote to his father from a hospital in St. Louis, Missouri. Although he describes his wounds as "not at all dangerous," Slatten, like so many suffering minor injuries, died soon after, probably from an infection.

occasion he missed the comforts of home. In February 1863, he wrote to his parents: "Some scamp stole my blanket when we were at Osage Springs, the night that it snowed so hard. ... We had no overcoats. ... I had to lie down on the frozen ground and take it. I was so tired that I dropped to sleep. ... When I awoke I was almost frozen. That was the only time I ever wished that I was back home. I would have given everything if I could only have been by our stove that night, and had a cup of warm coffee. I was very hungry, had had nothing to eat since morning."

After fighting in two skirmishes and one battle without injury, Jason Ellis, like so many soldiers, lost the battle against a different enemy—disease. He died of pleurisy in a Missouri hospital on February 28, 1863. James O'Bleness, who had a wife and seven children, was mortally wounded by a shot in the cheek on June 8, 1863, at the Battle of Milliken's Bend, Mississippi.

Before or after battle, if a photographer happened to be near the front, soldiers would find a moment to rest and pose for a portrait.

Perhaps the most famous of the Confederate ships was the Virginia, the former U.S. frigate Merrimack, which was converted into an armored gunboat, known as an "ironclad." The Virginia posed a significant threat to northern ships, but the Union soon built its own ironclad—the Monitor—and the two vessels faced each other in the world's first modern sea battle. While both sides claimed victory, the Virginia was permanently disabled; it never again attacked Union ships.

Approximately two hundred thousand black men served in the Union Army, but they were segregated and treated as second-class soldiers, receiving less pay and fewer provisions than white recruits.

The Union Navy, however, had difficulty filling its ranks and was more eager to enlist black men. It recruited twenty thousand black volunteers, and the limited space on ships made it impractical to separate black and white sailors. The men worked, ate, slept, and fought alongside one another, regardless of race.

But, the risks and monotony of soldering were not reserved for the infantry alone. When war broke out, Yankee and rebel alike swarmed to enlist—in the army. Few volunteers thought about joining the navy, and throughout the war both governments struggled to fill the ranks at sea.

When President Lincoln took office, the Union Navy had just forty-two ships on active duty, and most were stationed thousands of miles away. Still, the North had the upper hand: The Confederate States had no navy at all. The South quickly assembled a ragtag fleet, converting merchant vessels into warships, buying ships from Europe, and, when possible, building new ones.

But Union or Confederate, the sailor's life was one of routine—rising to reveille at five o'clock and quickly stowing one's gear in a hammock; then morning chores—washing the decks, polishing the brass, and cleaning the guns; and, finally, breakfast. The rest of the day was taken up with drills and more chores, broken up by mid-day and evening meals.

Sailors passed their free time much the same way as other soldiers—writing letters, talking, holding contests, and playing games; but, living in cramped quarters on the same ship for months at a time became painfully tedious. Those assigned to river gunboats had frequent opportunity to disembark, though their closeness to shore also made their position the most dangerous. Union sailors assigned to blockade duty in the South had the least dangerous and most monotonous duty—patrolling the same harbors and river entrances for months on end to prevent foreign vessels from bringing much-needed supplies to the Confederacy. ☆

MAKING DO

With a wealth of new land in the West and a growing immigrant population, the North learned to rely on its own people and resources. The South had trouble making the same transition; it had few factories to process its raw crops of cotton, corn, and tobacco.

Union troops blew up this Georgia Railroad roundhouse in Atlanta. For every train or set of tracks destroyed, hundreds of people would lose their connection to desperately needed goods.

Workers load bales of cotton in the busy southern port of Charleston, South Carolina, where early in the war activity was brought to a near standstill by a Union Navy blockade.

ONE OF THE GREATEST challenges for both the Union and Confederacy was supplying their armies with food, clothing, weapons, blankets, tents, and medical supplies, while still meeting the needs of people on the home front. When hundreds of thousands of men—farmers, bankers, store owners, and factory workers— left their jobs to fight, many of their positions were filled by people who remained behind: newly arrived immigrants, the very young and old, and women who had never worked outside the home before. But this depleted civilian work force struggled to produce and distribute goods.

In addition, the North and South had long relied on each other: The South had grown most of the country's crops and the North produced finished goods in its factories. When the war began and this balance was interrupted, the Confederate states suffered most. With a smaller population, limited railroad transportation, and few factories or mining operations, the South had a very difficult time both supplying its army and providing for its citizens.

Southerners were forced to devise creative methods to support the war effort. Citizens collected everything from lead window weights to brass church bells to melt down to make bullets, guns, and cannon. One such effort in Charleston, South Carolina, alone brought in 200,000 pounds of lead.

Yet, even when there were

The frenzied pace in northern factories led to poor workmanship. Many times uniforms and blankets would tear or unravel soon after they were issued to soldiers. Black volunteers, such as this member of Company E, 127th Ohio Colored Infantry, often received the poorest quality goods.

By seceding from the Union, the South put economic pressure on the North. Northern businesses lost a $300 million debt owed them by Southerners, which caused fears of financial disaster. But, to meet wartime demands, northern businesses churned out goods faster then ever. By the middle of 1862, the Union's economy had recovered.

"*Rats are a luxury. Small fishes sell at twenty dollars. Chickens at ten dollars each.... Mule meat has sold readily at two dollars per pound ... and I eat it once a week. The soldiers have had only one meal a day for ten days, and then one man does not get what a child should have.*"

A reporter for the *Augusta Daily Constitutionalist*, reporting on the plight of Confederate troops in the summer of 1863

To finance its war efforts, the South issued Federal bonds—loans in the form of paper money that the government promised to repay with interest after the war was won. But, the South did not win and the debt was never repaid. By 1865, inflation reached nine thousand percent. Confederate money was worth so little that one "dollar" was worth just a bit more than a penny!

adequate quantities of materials, quality was a serious problem. Stories were rampant of weapons not firing, powder not igniting, and bullets remaining lodged in gun barrels.

A major goal of the Union Navy was to blockade southern ports, stopping ships from delivering goods. The Union's efforts quickly took their toll on the South. In the fall of 1861, a Charleston merchant wrote that "everything [is] enormously high. Salt selling at 15 and 20 cents a quarter. Hardly any shoes to be had. Dry goods of every kind running out."

Some Southerners resorted to illegal trading across enemy lines. Those who were willing to risk the trip could sell a sack of salt that cost one dollar and twenty-five cents in the North for sixty dollars in the South; and cotton that sold for twenty cents a pound in Memphis or New Orleans could bring nearly two dollars a pound in New York.

Most people simply did their best to get by with what they had. As one southern woman wrote in her diary, "nothing is thrown away now." She proudly described how she turned a pair of old coat sleeves into shoes: "I cut an exact pattern from my old shoes, laid it on the sleeves, and cut out thus good uppers and sewed them carefully; . . . I am so proud of these home-made shoes, [I] think I'll put them in a glass case when the war is over."

While Union troops often had inadequate uniforms, supplies, and ammunition, the South had far greater problems; and, as the war raged on, conditions grew worse. By 1865, most Southerners were destitute and the country had a debt of two billion dollars. It would take years for the region to recover. ☆

FEAST OR FAMINE

The plump, well-dressed man in this Harper's Weekly cartoon is a beef contractor—a businessman who sold supplies to the army. Some contractors overcharged the government for poor-quality food, a strategy that undermined the health and comfort of the soldiers who were fighting for them.

Broadway Landing, on the Appomattox River, was a supply depot for Federal troops. One of the greatest challenges the government faced was coordinating large shipments of food and supplies for troops who were constantly on the move.

> *"**N**o rations have been issued for two or three days and then but half allowance. We have been compelled to grate corn for mush and bread or go hungry; I grated corn [for] a couple of hours yesterday."*
>
> **Alonzo Wardall, January 1863**
> **Company I, Third Iowa Infantry**

"**I**T IS THIS WAY WITH us, *feast* or *famine*," wrote one Union soldier in a letter to his parents. During much of the war, Union and Confederate soldiers alike suffered through days with no rations issued; when shipments of food finally caught up to them, the famished men consumed two or three days' worth of meals at once, then waited anxiously for their next rations.

Overall, northern regiments were much better supplied than their southern counterparts. Union soldiers lived mainly on a diet of salt pork, bread, beans, and coffee. They supplemented their rations with cakes and pies bought from sutlers—peddlers who followed troops from camp to camp. In addition, families and aid societies in the North sent the troops thousands of boxes containing smoked meats, pies, dried fruits, and jams, although much of it spoiled by the time it reached the men.

As they trudged through the countryside, soldiers on both sides foraged for food, hunting wild animals, such as birds and deer, gathering berries, and picking fruit from orchards. On many occasions, hungry soldiers raided homes and farms, taking food from kitchens and storerooms, and stealing chickens, pigs, cows, and sheep from barns and pastures.

Foraged food was a welcome addition to a soldier's diet. Union or Confederate, army rations were typically

TEETH DULLERS AND WORM CASTLES

Hardtack. The mere mention of it could send chills up and down a soldier's spine. These flour-and-water biscuits, issued to Union soldiers, were baked to last. However, by the time shipments reached the troops, the crackers more closely resembled concrete than bread. Soldiers soon referred to them by nicknames such as "teeth dullers" and "sheet-iron crackers."

One veteran recalled that army regulations stated "a good set of teeth were necessary for a recruit on account of the necessity of biting the end of the paper cartridge [when loading shot into a rifle], but for this it appeared that only front teeth were required. . . . But when . . . that wonderful creation . . . known as the army cracker appeared, this mystery of the requirement of the teeth was fully cleared up. It then appeared that men were selected not for courage or endurance . . . , but for good grinders."

Soldiers had no choice but to survive as best they could on hardtack. Dipping the stale, moldy hard bread in coffee or soup softened it, but also loosened the worms and weevils that typically infested it.

So bad was the problem of worm infestation that soldiers came to call the crackers "worm castles." As one disgruntled man put it, "All the fresh meat we had came in the hard bread."

bland at best, unpalatable at worst. Worms and weevils infested bread and other foods, and spoiled meat was a common sight. In addition, soldiers fried most of their meals in grease, causing numerous stomach ailments.

One thing Northerners and Southerners shared was a love for coffee. Northern soldiers usually had plentiful supplies, and some men drank as many as four or five quarts a day.

In the South, coffee beans were often scarce for both soldiers and civilians. When they ran low, Southerners mixed in chicory or other spices to stretch the beans they had, or substituted rye, corn meal, peanuts, acorns, beets, or sweet potatoes for coffee beans. Since cream was often unavailable, some people mixed in egg whites or butter instead.

Few Southerners had anticipated the severe shortages. In October 1862, one well-to-do woman in Vicksburg, Mississippi, wrote in her diary that there was no scarcity of "butter, hives for honey, and no end to pigs. Chickens seem to be kept like game in parks . . . and eggs are plentiful." Her family of ten had chicken for breakfast, lunch, and supper—"fried, stewed, broiled, and in soup"—and "the only privations . . . [were] the lack of coffee, tea, salt, matches, and good candles."

A cook for the Army of the Potomac prepares a meal in the winter of 1864. With a limited variety of ingredients and crude facilities, one meal often tasted the same as the next.

The soldiers' fare is very rough,
The bread is hard, the beef is tough;
If they can stand it, it will be,
Through love of God, a mystery.

Written by a Union soldier
and printed in the
Nashville *Daily Union*, April 16, 1863

"For God sake do come home. I am sick. There is nothing in the house to live on…. The cows got in, and ate up the garden, and everything has gone to the devil and you jist have to come."

Amanda, the wife of an Illinois volunteer,
in a letter to her husband

In his makeshift camp, a soldier boils a pot of coffee and stakes a small piece of meat over the fire for dinner.

A CIVIL WAR MENU

• Salt Horse •

A slang term for salted beef issued by the northern army. It was so salty, it was said to last as long as two years before decaying. Soldiers soaked it for hours before they could stand to eat it, a process that took away the flavor as well as the nutrients.

• Cush •

A Confederate stew made with bacon, cornbread, and water, cooked until the water evaporated.

• Essence of Coffee •

This first instant coffee was introduced during the Civil War. Soldiers tried their best to dissolve the pasty, unappetizing substance in cups of campfire-heated water, but the mixture, shipped in tin cans and likened in texture to axle grease, never caught on in popularity.

• Artificial Oysters •

A southern concoction of grated green corn mixed with egg and butter, then rolled and fried. It had the texture of fried oysters, if not the flavor.

• Desiccated Potatoes •

These and other dried vegetables such as carrots, beets, turnips, string beans, and onions were distributed to Federal troops under the notion that they helped prevent scurvy. The dried slabs, heavily seasoned with pepper, were described as looking like "a dirty brook with dead leaves floating around" when they were made into soup.

• Bully Soup •

A northern hot cereal consisting of cornmeal, crushed hardtack, wine, ginger, and water all cooked together.

• Skillygalee •

A Yankee name for hardtack soaked in water, then browned in pork fat.

• Lobscouse •

Invented by sailors, this dish was pork-flavored soup, thickened with hardtack.

But less than a year later, in May 1863, with provisions growing scarcer, she subsisted mainly on "rice and milk." The monotonous diet became almost unbearable to her: "I am so tired of corn-bread that I eat it with tears in my eyes."

As Union troops invaded the South, many plantation owners lost their homes, their livestock, and their crops. By 1863, thousands of Southerners were facing famine.

People settled for whatever nourishment they could find. In her diary, the same woman in Vicksburg wrote that her servant, Martha, had returned from her daily shopping to report that "rats are hanging dressed in the market for sale with mule-meat: There is nothing else [to be found]."

The Confederate Congress had tried to curb the shortages by passing a resolution calling for farmers to plant edible crops, instead of cotton and tobacco. Though food became somewhat more plentiful, storage and transport problems grew worse as Union troops destroyed buildings, railroads, ships, and roads. On many occasions, food rotted at railway stations awaiting the arrival of trains that never came. And even when transportation ran smoothly, the movement of troops, weapons, and ammunition took priority over the shipment of civilian food.

Shortages of food were so severe that many Confederate soldiers deserted, returning home to help their families. ☆

A PATH OF DESTRUCTION

All that remains of this ammunition train are dozens of charred wheels. Forced to retreat, Confederate General John Bell Hood ordered his own troops to destroy it—and the factory beside the tracks—rather than leave the supplies for the advancing Union Army.

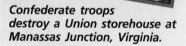

Confederate troops destroy a Union storehouse at Manassas Junction, Virginia.

One of the keys to the success of the Union Army was its broad network of railroads, which allowed for efficient movement of troops and supplies. Union troops concentrated on destroying southern railroads, which cut off the Confederates from desperately needed provisions and reinforcements.

WHEN THEY WERE ON THE march—and cut off from supply lines—the Union and Confederate armies soon discovered they could survive by living off the land they crossed. Without the added weight of extra rations, the soldiers moved quickly and lightly. Instead of relying on army provisions, they ransacked homes for what they needed. Civilians soon discovered no one and nothing was safe. As southern reporter Ben Lane Posey wrote, "It matters little whether the Yankee army or ours visits them. The result is the same—they are ruined."

Yet, as Union soldiers marched through the South, they had a clear mission: Destroy the enemy and end the war. The troops created a path of destruction, decimating plantations, farmhouses, slave quarters, and fields of crops. They bombarded cities, reducing hotels, stores, railroad stations, churches, and houses to rubble. In the process, they ruined the homes and lives of tens of thousands of Southerners.

In the fall of 1864, Union General Philip Sheridan reported on his successes in Virginia's Shenandoah Valley. "I have destroyed over two thousand barns filled with wheat and hay and farming implements, over seventy mills filled with flour and wheat; have driven in front of the army

Southern troops were unable to halt the march on Atlanta. They dug miles of trenches, built earth-reinforced bunkers, and planted sharpened stakes as barriers to hinder the Union soldiers. But where Union troops couldn't storm through, they marched around, leaving behind useless fortifications and abandoned buildings. Northern cannon fire destroyed hundreds of homes like the one pictured here.

Runaway slaves, referred to as "contraband," or enemy property, were granted freedom by Lincoln's Emancipation Proclamation in September 1862. Free blacks still faced difficult times behind northern lines. Many had to rely on donations of food, clothing, and housing, none of which were plentiful.

Refugees, people who lost their homes during the war, often had little more than the clothes on their backs. Many traveled north, hoping to start a new life. Although the northern economy was thriving in comparison to the South's, refugees had a difficult time finding homes and jobs in an unfriendly land.

NEGRO PASSPORT.
CONFEDERATE STATES OF AMERICA, WAR DEP'T,

Pass

Richmond,

to

1865.

By

Subject to the discretion of the Military authorities.

DESCRIPTION.—Age

, Height   Provost Marshal.

, Color

In the South, slaves routinely went from town to town, or plantation to plantation, running errands and doing odd jobs for their owners; but their travel was controlled. Without a pass, a slave was considered a runaway and was arrested or shot. When the Union Army began allowing black men to volunteer for service, slaveowners became even more watchful.

over four thousand head of stock, and have killed and issued to the troops not less than three thousand sheep."

Many residents fled as Union troops approached. They crowded trains, filled carts drawn by mules or oxen, and traveled on foot, carrying with them as many of their belongings as they could. "Everybody has left [Petersburg], or is preparing to leave, who is able to get away," reported Peter W. Alexander in the summer of 1864. "The houses, and even the woods and fields, for miles around . . . are filled with women and children and old men. . . . This is a sad fate for a town so distinguished. . . ."

After the "terrible fire that destroyed most of Columbia," E. P. Burton, a Union surgeon, described a similar scene: "All around the outskirts of the city were groups of women and children sitting on . . . all that was left them. All looked tired—many crying and despondent . . . some complaining terribly about the Yankees."

The soldiers broke into stores of liquor and became drunk, he continued, "and then they run riot all night . . . [and] robbed and pillaged both houses and citizens."

Some people escaped the shelling and devastation to live with relatives or friends in other towns, but many left their homes only to find themselves in unfamiliar land with no shelter or food. Mrs. John A. Logan, a northern woman traveling with her husband's troops through the South, recalled seeing the "poor, helpless creatures, black and white, . . . under the woodsheds on the [railroad] line . . . with nothing but a few clothes and little bundles of

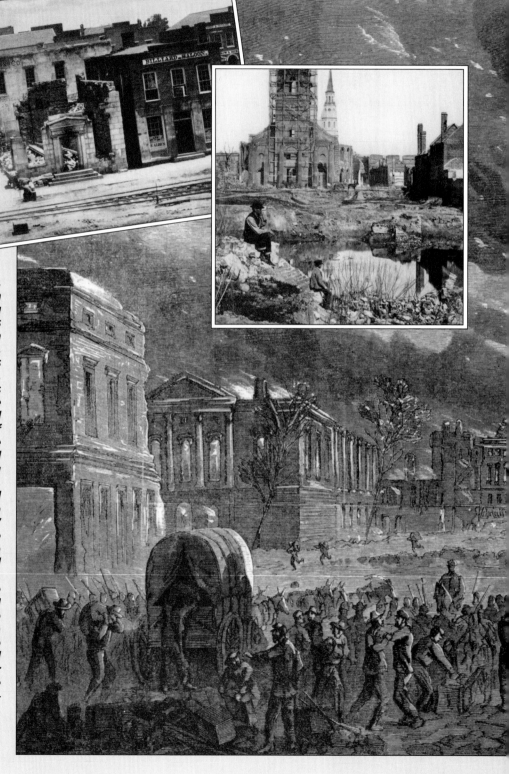

On February 16, 1865, E. P. Burton, a surgeon traveling with Sherman's army, sat down with his diary. Recalling the day's events, he wrote, "Two or three miles distant were the steeples and chimneys of Columbia. The valley was covered with moving columns of soldiers. . . . The whole field was glistening with bright bayonets." Two days later, the town, shown in the background illustration here, had burned to the ground, "a sight I hope to never see again," Burton wrote. From left to right, the charred remains of other major cities of the Confederacy—Atlanta, Charleston, and Richmond.

bedding and articles of household belongings. Sick, destitute, homeless, friendless, and among strangers . . . their condition was unutterably sad."

One by one, southern cities surrendered: New Orleans in April 1862; Atlanta in September 1864; Columbia in February 1865; and, finally, Petersburg and Richmond in April 1865. Southerners caught in the chaos watched as Confederate troops retreated and Union forces moved in.

"Just before dawn explosions of gunboats . . . shook the city, and glass was shattered, and new houses crumbled," wrote Mrs. Mary A. Fontaine as General Grant's Union troops attacked Richmond. "Immense fires stretched their arms on high all around me. . . . I watched two blue figures on the Capitol . . . saw them unfurl a tiny flag [at City Hall], and then I sank on my knees, and the bitter, bitter tears came in a torrent."

In a letter to her cousin, Fontaine went on to describe the uproar: "Imagine the streets crowded with . . . troops by the thousands, some loaded with plunder from burning stores . . . dozens of bands trying to drown each other . . . men shouting and swearing as I never heard men do before." And all the while, "the fire [was] creeping steadily nearer to us . . . the heavens were black as with a thunder cloud, [and] great pieces of shells [were] flying about."

For civilians caught in the tumult of war, surviving daily life became as fierce a struggle as that faced by the soldiers on the battlefield. ☆

A WORLD OF DEATH

After the Battle of Antietam, on September 17, 1862, bodies of soldiers lay strewn across the banks of Antietam Creek and scattered through the surrounding woods and cornfields. The armies led by Union General George B. McClellan and Confederate General Robert E. Lee fought what was the single bloodiest day of the war: The Union had more than twelve thousand casualties, the Confederates ten thousand. All told, close to twenty-three thousand soldiers were missing, injured, or dead.

Families of missing soldiers would sometimes search battlefields and hospitals, hoping to find their loved ones alive, but ready to face the news if they were dead. Dr. Richard Briggs' embalming business, pictured here, prepared bodies for burial.

THE CASUALTIES.

List of Killed, Wounded and Missing in the Second Vermont Brigade, Third Division, First Army Corps, in the Battles of the 2d and 3d July instant.
We are indebted to Mr. GEORGE H. BIGELOW, proprietor of the Burlington *Daily Times*, and Acting Quartermaster of the Twelfth Vermont regiment, for the following list (nearly complete) of the casualties of the Vermont brigade.

Brig.-Gen. G. J. Stannard —leg.

Capt. A. C. Foster, Ins.-Gen. Staff—leg.

THIRTEENTH REGIMENT.

Lt.-Col. W. D. Munson—slightly.
Sergt. Maj. H. H. Smith—killed.
1st Lieut. John T. Sennott, Co. A— mortally.
Sergt. Thos. Blake, Co. A—mortally.
John Shanaghan, Co. A—mortally.
John Cane, Co. A—missing.
J. Bruin, Co. A—missing.
J. Catlan, Co. A—missing.
Anthony Donnelly, Co. A—missing.
J. Herigan, Co. A—missing.
C. M. Nellis, Co. A—missing.
P. R. Reddy, Co. A—missing.
W. Woodrutte, Co. A—miss'g.
J. H. Wilson, Co. B—killed.
S. G. Dana, Co. B—severely.
D. Parker, Co. B—severely.
A. H. Chase, Co. B—severely.
J. Simmons, Co. C—sev'ly.
H. Martin, Co. C—sev'ly.
S. W. Benjamin, Co. C—sli.
J. S. Caswell, Co. C—slight.
A. Nye, Co. C—slight.
W. C. Snow, Co. C—slight.
H. Wakefield, Co. C—slight.
C. Watson, Co. C—slightly.
H. Miles, Co. C—slightly.
G. Pierce, Co. C—missing.
V. Genart, Co. C—missing.
O. Marseill, Co. D—killed.
W. Morch, Co. D—killed.
Sergt. J. F. Dinsmore, Co. D— wounded, severely.
Corp. J. M. Chapin, Co. E—severely.
Corp. D. Butler, Co. E—severely.
D. M. Dickenson, Co. E—severely.
W. Whitney, Co. E—severely.
John Hull, Co. E—severely.
Sergt. J. D. Catlin, Co. E—slightly.
J. Daniels, Co. E—slightly.
L. G. Seely, Co E—slightly.
S. O. Wells, Co. E—slightly.
S. C. Sanborn, Co. E—slightly.
Corp. Henry Russell, Co. F—killed.
Corp. Geo. F. Baldwin, Co. F— wounded severely.
— Lawrence, Co. F—slightly.

F. Corey, Co. A—killed.
Michael McAnerny, Co. A—mortally.
M. Mulloy, Co. A—mortally.
Corp. T. W. Sibley, Co. A—severely.
J. Hanlou, Co. A—severely.
A. Guinett, Co. A—severely.
P. Monaghan, Co. A—seve'ly.
J. Wallace, Co. A—severely.
Corp. J. Dolph, Co. B—slight.
D. L. Stoddard, Co. B—slight.
C. Carpenter, Co. B—slightly.
Z. Keyes, Co. B—slightly.
O. G. Mills, Co. B—slightly.
L. K. Dow, Co. B—slightly.
J. W. Richardson, Co. B—sli'y
G. Stoddard, Co. B—missing.
E. A. Fiske, Co. B—missing.
Color Sergt. D. A. Marbie, Co. C— severely.
J. E. Baliou, Co. C—severely.
S. S. Pratt, Co. C—severely.
Sergt. J. Harmon, Co. D—severely.
L. M. Bently, Co. D—sev.
M. P. Scullin, Co. D—sev.
Corp. R. G. Griffin, Co. D—slightly.
W. Crosby, Co. D—slightly.
John Johnson, Co. D—slight.
H. Tomlinson, Co. D—slight.
G. W. Lee, Co. D—slightly.
O. S. Kerr, Co. E—killed.
Lieut. F. Kenfield, Co. D—wounded, severely.
Corp. C. Woelcot, Co. E—wounded, severely.
Thos. Sneil, Co. G—severely.
Corp. Geo. Cutting, Co. G—slight.
Jude Nowcity, Co.G—slight.
John Tague, Co. G—severe.
Wm. Warner, Co. G—slight.
Henry Heath, Co. G—slight.
Corp. James L. Martin, Co. H— dangerous.
Andrew E. Osgood, Co. H—slight.
Wm. Roak, Co. H—slight.
Nelson Cattaract, Co. H—slight.
H. Wilson, Co. H—slight.
B. W. Wright, Co. I—dangerous.
C. E. Seaver, Co

*This clipping from the **New York Times** lists the casualties from just one regiment at the Battle of Gettysburg. During the first three days of July 1863, there were 51,112 casualties at the Pennsylvania battlesite. Almost one of every three men was injured or killed.*

During the war, nearly every American lost a family member. After a battle, people would worriedly scan lists of the dead, wounded, and missing printed in the local newspaper or posted outside the telegraph office.

Aᴀᴛᴇʀ ᴛʜᴇ Bᴀᴛᴛʟᴇ OF Shiloh, General William Tecumseh Sherman wrote that he gazed upon "piles of dead soldiers' mangled bodies . . . without heads and legs" and thought "the scenes on this field would have cured anybody of war."

But they did not. It was April 1862 and the country had been at war for one year. At Shiloh alone, there were twenty thousand casualties, and the killing would continue for three more years. By April 1865, 623,000 men had died in the War Between the States.

When North faced South, soldiers sometimes fought hand to hand with fists, gun butts, swords, and bayonets, but more often the two sides blazed away, firing muskets at each other from just a few hundred yards apart. In battle after battle, tens of thousands of bullets tore in every direction, decimating soldiers.

Afterward, the air would be filled with the smoky haze of gunfire as the companies of men regrouped and assessed their losses. When there were too many casualties to bury them individually, they placed dead soldiers in mass graves.

Reverend J. B. Rogers, a Union Army chaplain, noted that it was "[his] lot to attend the burial of many whose names were unknown." He described how they wrapped the dead in their blankets and buried them: "Why without coffins? Because there are

This field map of the area surrounding Atlanta was found on the body of Union General James McPherson—stained with his blood. He was shot by enemy rifle fire outside the city in 1864. When possible, survivors sent personal belongings of the dead such as diaries, letters, and photographs to their next of kin; but soldiers had few qualms about taking food and clothing from deceased men, especially if it meant saving other lives.

In May 1863, at Fredericksburg, Virginia, Captain A. J. Russell photographed the Union troops, above, waiting to be called to battle and this sunken road, left, littered with bodies of fallen soldiers.

none at hand, and none to make them. Each regiment has enough to do in burying its own dead. . . . They only have time to dig a grave . . . even this being . . . no light tax."

Those who witnessed death firsthand would never forget the experience. "Stretched out in every direction, as far as the eye could reach, were the dead and dying," wrote Mrs. John Harris, a nurse from Philadelphia, after the Battle of Cedar Mountain, Virginia, in August 1862. "Much the larger proportion must have died instantly—their positions, some with ramrod in hand to load, others with gun in hand as if about to aim, others still having just discharged their murderous load. Some were struck in the act of eating. One poor fellow still held a potato in his grasp. Another clutched a piece of tobacco; others held their canteens as if to drink; one grasped a letter. Two were strangely poised upon a fence, having been killed in the act of leaping it."

For many, it was difficult to ignore the memories of what they saw. After attending a Richmond dinner party in February 1864, Confederate General John C. Breckinridge remarked, "I have asked myself more than once tonight: 'Are you the same man who stood gazing down on the faces of the dead on that awful battlefield; the soldiers lying there . . . with their eyes wide open. Is this the same world?'" ☆

Of the three million Americans who fought in the war, 234,000 died of battle wounds, and even more—an astounding 388,580—perished from disease.

THE SICK AND WOUNDED

Both armies had limited means of caring for men wounded in battle. After being carried off the field, soldiers were loaded on horse-drawn ambulances and specially equipped hospital trains. Bounced and jostled painfully over dirt roads and railroad tracks, many died on the way to the hospital.

By 1863, the Union Army had improved its ambulance corps, requiring that each wagon be supplied with two leather-covered benches for wounded men, two kegs of water, a supply of beef broth, bandages, and stretchers. Still, the rides were rough and the survival rate low; soldiers referred even to the improved ambulances as "dead carts."

The Fifty-seventh New York Ambulance Corps practices gathering wounded soldiers near Culpeper, Virginia, in 1863.

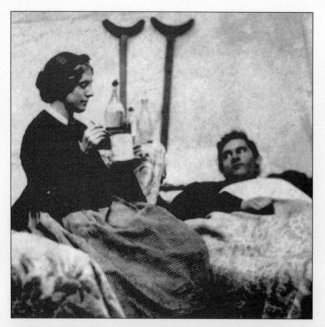

As the Union Army pushed deeper into the South, conditions for the wounded grew worse. After battles, any available buildings—churches, hotels, warehouses, shops, barns, and homes—were used to house the wounded and dying. Few were as clean and well equipped as this Union hospital in Tennessee.

In addition to trains and ambulances, the armies used riverboats to transport wounded men. Pictured here is the Nashville, a Union steamboat.

In October 1863, Riley Hoskinson, a Union soldier stationed in Chattanooga, Tennessee, wrote to his wife that he and their son, Stuart, had been ordered to assist the surgeons at a field hospital. "The wounded were coming in by scores, wounded in all parts of their bodies, from the top of the head to the ends of the toes . . . several shot in the mouth, one right through . . . into the groin."

Hoskinson went on to describe how he and Stuart "helped to carry them from the Ambulances to places of safety, then made fires to help keep them warm as the houses were all full. We made fires in the yard, in the garden and in the woods . . . Every Where we could find a place to put a man for comfort."

In the aftermath of battle, such chaotic scenes were common. Both sides struggled to remove severely wounded men from the scene of fighting and tend to their many needs.

After the Battle of Chantilly, Virginia, Clara Barton, a nurse who earned fame for her bravery and ingenuity, described how wounded men were "laid on the ground beside the train and so back up the hill 'till they covered acres." There was no place to shelter them, so she and the other nurses spread hay for bedding. "By midnight there must have been *three thousand* helpless men lying in that hay," she remarked. "All

In performing amputations, many surgeons feared that anesthetics were too dangerous for patients. Some used chloroform, which put a patient to sleep as he inhaled it, but many provided only a sip of whiskey and a strong man to hold the patient down. Above, a group of Union Army surgeons pose for a photograph.

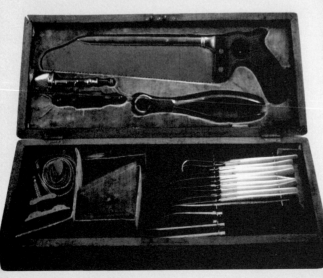

This Civil War medical kit was designed for a surgeon's frequent needs. It holds a saw for amputating limbs and a pliers-like instrument for removing bullets.

Clara Barton, a government clerk, organized her own nursing and supply operation to care for wounded soldiers.

Dorothea Dix, a reformer of mental hospitals, worked tirelessly as superintendent of the Union nursing corps during the war.

Louisa May Alcott volunteered as a wartime nurse in Washington, D.C., and later became a successful writer. Her best-known novel, Little Women, was the story of four northern sisters during the war.

night we made compresses and slings—and bound up and wet wounds, when we could get water, fed what we could, travelled miles in that dark over these poor helpless wretches, in terror lest some one's candle *fall into* the hay and consume them all."

Even when soldiers made it to a hospital, unsanitary conditions prevailed. Most doctors, unaware of the dangers of germs and bacteria, did not change out of dirty, blood-stained clothing or disinfect their equipment between operations. They used the same tools for hours, or even days, cleaning them with just a wipe on a towel or rag.

Thousands of men died from infections. With no antibiotics to help ward off infection, doctors often chose to amputate a wounded limb rather than risk losing the patient.

As one nurse, Belle Reynolds, observed after the Battle of Shiloh, "one by one they would take from different parts of the hospital a poor fellow, lay him out on those bloody boards, and administer chloroform; but before . . . the patient was fully asleep, the operation would begin, and in the midst of shrieks, curses, and wild laughs, the surgeon would wield over his wretched victim the glittering knife and saw; and soon the severed and ghastly limb, white as snow and spattered with blood, would fall upon the floor—one more added to the terrible pile."

Surgeons, nurses, and fellow soldiers enlisted to help with amputations soon became accustomed to the gruesome events. "Strange as it may seem to you," Hoskinson wrote to his wife, "I can now stand and hold one of a man's legs while the other is cut off and not feel the least particle of

Anxious to help the soldiers to victory, people on the home front formed aid societies, which gathered canned and dried food and homemade socks, underwear, and bandages to send to the troops. Their efforts to keep the soldiers well clothed and well fed most likely saved thousands of lives.

Established in 1861, the United States Sanitary Commission, a volunteer organization, provided health information, medical supplies, and care for wounded soldiers. With an office in Washington, D.C., and branches throughout the North, the commission raised money by selling donated items—everything from baked goods to farm machinery—at large events called Sanitary Fairs.

My Dear Friend,—You are not my husband nor son; but you are the husband or son of some woman who undoubtedly loves you as I love mine. I have made these garments for you with a heart that aches for your sufferings. . . .

Dear Soldiers,—The little girls of —— send this box to you. They hear that thirteen thousand of you are sick, and have been wounded in battle. They are very sorry, and want to do something for you. They cannot do much, for they are all small; but they have bought with their own money, and made what is in here. They hope it will do some good, and that you will all get well and come home.

My Dear Boy,—I have knit these socks expressly for you. How do you like them? How do you look, and where do you live when you are at home? I am nineteen years old, of medium height, of slight build, with blue eyes, fair complexion, light hair, and a good deal of it. Write and tell me all about yourself, and how you get on in the hospitals.

P. S. If the recipient of these socks has a wife, will he please exchange socks with some poor fellow not so fortunate?

My Brave Friend,—I have learned to knit on purpose to knit socks for the soldiers. This is my fourth pair. . . . Write to me, and tell me how you like the foot-gear and what we can do for you. Keep up good courage, and by and by you will come home to us.

When preparing "comfort bags," small packages of food and clothing for the soldiers, women and children often enclosed encouraging notes such as these written by members of aid societies in the Midwest.

that faintish disposition that troubled me so much in former life."

Hospital workers had to have strong nerves, and a stronger stomach. In addition, they faced long hours washing and bandaging wounds, dispensing meals and medicine, and comforting dying men. More than three thousand women served as nurses during the war; despite protests from many doctors that women were too delicate for the profession, the female nurses proved they were up to the challenge.

But, North or South, hospital life was far from pleasant. Hoskinson described the atmosphere as "much like that of a lively revival meeting where many pray in a low tone . . . 'O Lord,' 'O My God,' 'Lord Save,' . . . commingled with incoherent cries and groans . . . day and night, with the additions of the wants, such as, 'I want up,' . . . 'I want some medicine,' 'I want my wound dressed,' . . . 'I am too hot,' 'I am too cold,' 'Doctor how long can I live?' 'How long must I lie thus?'"

Soldiers on both sides fought some of their most difficult battles against common enemies: infection, diarrhea, smallpox, typhoid, scurvy, malaria, and dysentery. In the end, more men died from infection or disease than from battle wounds.

Rather than a quick and glorious death so many had imagined for themselves at the start of the war, soldiers were worn down by long marches, poor diets, and exposure to wind, rain, snow, and sun. Whether Union or Confederate, a soldier's worst enemies were lack of medical knowledge, inadequate shelter, and limited supplies. ☆

PRISONERS OF WAR

At Andersonville Prison, open ditches served as toilets. Filled with raw sewage, they ran directly into creeks where prisoners drew drinking water. The result of the contamination was widespread illness, including dysentery, a disorder that caused severe diarrhea and, for many, brought death.

Fellow prisoners bury the dead side by side in a shallow trench at Andersonville.

The interior fence—known as the "dead line"—enforced the simplest of laws: To cross it or lean on it meant instant death. Even laying a hand on it brought a bullet from the sharpshooters in the guard towers. Many men accidentally strayed too close and were killed.

"The air of the prison seemed putrid; . . . filth covered the ground; . . . no shelter was furnished beyond what could be constructed of blankets or garments. All my former experience of prison life had not prepared me for such unmitigated misery as met me everywhere."

Warren Lee Goss, Second Massachusetts Regiment of Heavy Artillery, on arriving at Andersonville Prison

ONE OF THE GREATEST atrocities of the Civil War was the treatment of prisoners of war. The South, which could not afford to clothe and feed its own soldiers and civilians, could hardly do better for enemy prisoners. Yet, in the North, too, prisons became overcrowded and disease-ridden.

According to Harriet Hawley, a Union nurse working in North Carolina, "No human tongue or pen [could] describe the horrible condition which [the prisoners] were in. Starving to death, covered with vermin, with no clothing but the filthy rags they had worn during their whole imprisonment—a period of from five to twenty months; cramped by long sitting in one position, so that they could not straighten their limbs; their feet rotted off!"

Neither the Union nor the Confederacy had expected to house and feed thousands of enemy soldiers. The men were confined in a variety of makeshift prisons—factories, military barracks, schools, warehouses, and open-air stockades—while political leaders argued over a fair way to exchange them. The soldiers were fed uncooked beans or cornmeal, given dirty water to drink, and provided little or no medical care. In addition to wounds they suffered in battle before being captured, their poor diets and filthy surroundings made them easily susceptible to the many diseases that penetrated the camps.

The most infamous of all Civil War

TO COLORED MEN!

FREEDOM,

Protection, Pay, and a Call to Military Duty!

On the 1st day of January, 1863, the President of the United States proclaimed FREE-DOM to over THREE MILLIONS OF SLAVES. This decree is to be enforced by all the power of the Nation. On the 21st of July last he issued the following order:

PROTECTION OF COLORED TROOPS.

"WAR DEPARTMENT, ADJUTANT GENERAL'S OFFICE,
WASHINGTON, July 21.

Early in the war, the Union and Confederacy temporarily traded prisoners of war under a prearranged system—a lieutenant for four privates, a commanding general for sixty privates, and so on. But in 1863, the Confederacy became angry that black men (many of whom were former slaves) were fighting for the Union, and refused to exchange black soldiers. President Lincoln called off all exchanges, demanding that soldiers be traded by the agreed-upon system, regardless of race. The Confederacy refused to compromise until January 1865, giving both armies the unexpected burden of housing and feeding thousands of prisoners of war.

These three Confederate soldiers were taken as prisoners after the Battle of Gettysburg in 1863. Their casual, mismatched clothing was typical of southern soldiers after two years of war.

Few men expected to be imprisoned for long, but their "temporary" situations stretched into years. Through frosty winter nights, spring rainstorms, and summer heat spells, they wore what few clothes they brought with them to threads.

To recapture escaped prisoners, guards used dogs, such as this Russian bloodhound named Hero, to hunt the men down.

Their clothing worn to shreds, these Union prisoners wearily and anxiously wait to be exchanged with Confederate prisoners.

prisons was Andersonville. The sixteen-acre Georgia stockade camp was originally intended to hold ten thousand men. But as prisoners poured in, the camp was expanded by ten acres. By August 1864, just six months after the prison opened, thirty-three thousand men were housed in what was little more than a large dirt field.

Enclosed by a double line of wooden fences, the prison consisted of hills of open ground. It had no buildings to house the men and no trees to shade them from the sweltering summer heat. During cold and rainy weather, men huddled together for warmth—many had no tents, only torn blankets or tattered clothing to protect them.

By 1865, forty thousand northern prisoners had been brought to Andersonville, and thirteen thousand died there—more than a hundred men a day in the summer of 1864.

Near the end of the war, as both sides began releasing prisoners, civilians were horrified to see the sick and emaciated men. One woman described the survivors as "strange, skeleton men, in tattered, faded blue," while another recalled that released prisoners were "so restless and wild looking; others . . . had placidly vacant faces, as if they had been dead to the world for years."

The treatment of prisoners of war took a huge toll: Of the 214,000 Confederate prisoners held in the North during the war, 26,000 died. And, in the South, where 194,000 Union soldiers had been imprisoned, more than 30,000 men perished.

For Americans, north and south, perhaps the most startling evidence of the serious consequences of civil war was the horrific condition of the prisoners. ☆

WRITING HOME

C. W. Edwards, a Union soldier, wrote to his cousin in January 1865 while recuperating in a Washington, D.C., hospital: "I have been out twice on a pass and I saw a good many things that were new to me. I visited the Capitol, the Patent Office, the Post Office and the Smithsonian . . . , which I think beats them all." In his excitement to describe the new sights, Edwards wrote the letter quickly; note that he apologizes for his "bad writing."

By 1863, southern paper supplies were running low. People continued to write, using small, cramped handwriting on whatever scraps of paper they could find. Rather than sending separate letters to people at home, it was common for a soldier to ask the recipient—his mother, brother, or girlfriend—to pass the letter along to others.

Letters were the lifeblood of the war for soldiers away from home. Writing to family and friends, they described the food they ate and the clothes they wore, landscape they passed and weather they endured. They wrote about new friends and the enemy troops they faced. Many described the terrible fear that ran through their veins when finally, after months of waiting, they entered battle.

When that time came, it often passed in a blur—thousands of men yelling and swarming at one another, cannon and rifle fire exploding in deafening sounds, injured men shrieking in pain, and bodies being ripped apart. Many had trouble finding words to describe the awful scenes. "No correspondence can describe the fighting there on Saturday morning," wrote Major Robert Lusby, a Union soldier, after the Battle of Corinth, Mississippi, in October 1862. "I don't believe any man ever saw more desperate, reckless, and brave charges than the enemy made on our guns. . . . I never saw anything so grand and awful before."

Such letters gave civilians an impression of the horrors of war, from

April 11, 1865

My Dear Little Daughter Ida,

I am glad you have got over your sick spell. I hope you will keep well and grow and get fat by the time I get home. Be a nice girl. Take good care of Georgie. Tell him that Par is coming home one of these days and bring him a big apple. I have got that little Bag and needle Book and scissors you made for me yet. Be kind and pleasant to all the little girls when you meet with them and then they will love you. You must print me a letter when you have time and tell me lots of news.

J. H. Mitchell
(rank, company unknown)

During the Civil War, mail was shipped by train and horse-drawn wagons. Union soldiers often had long waits between deliveries, but, in time, their correspondence usually got through. The Confederate postal service, however, was highly unreliable. To avoid paying postage for a letter that might never be delivered, soldiers would ask camp visitors or men on furlough to carry letters back home with them.

April 8, 1864

Dear Brother,

The great fight is over, and I am still in the land of the living; which is more than I can say of thousands who were well on Sunday morning. We arrived here on Friday night last, and on Sunday at 10 A.M., we were led into the fight. To give you a description of the battle would take more paper than I have at my command. . . . Our regiment lost about 150 in killed and wounded. . . . I never received a scratch, but such a whistling of balls was not desirable to hear. I was over the field of battle the next day, and have no anxiety to go over it again. It was a horrible sight; but a soldier soon gets used to anything.

Madison R. Laird
Lieutenant, Company F, 16th Iowa Infantry
(after Battle of Shiloh)

people they knew and in words they understood. And, more important still, if they received a letter, it meant that the loved one who wrote it was still alive.

Soldiers also longed for news from friends, wives, girlfriends, parents, and siblings, though it often took weeks or more for mail to catch up to a soldier whose regiment was zigzagging from one assignment to the next. "The mails bring me letters very slowly," wrote Charles Blackford, a Confederate soldier, in a letter to his daughter Nannie. "I have been nearly a month in this strange land amongst strangers—almost a thousand miles away—and have only one letter to tell me whether you and your mother are dead or alive."

When mail arrived at the front, letters and packages from home immediately lifted the spirits of soldiers, just as a lack of mail would add to the gloom. "We get the blues sometimes . . . worn out with duty, wet, and muddy. The coffee is bad, the crackers worse, the bacon worst of all; and we are as hungry as wolves," described one soldier. "Just then the mail boy brings in a letter— a good one from you, or from mother. Immediately all the weariness is gone . . . the musty, fusty, rusty crackers and bacon are better; and I am just the happiest fellow in all the world." ☆

NEWS OF THE WAR

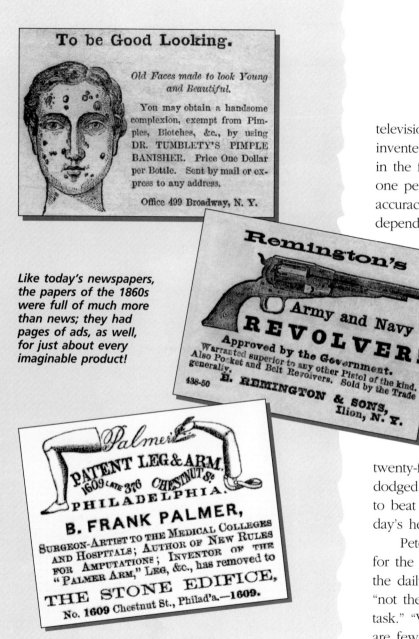

Like today's newspapers, the papers of the 1860s were full of much more than news; they had pages of ads, as well, for just about every imaginable product!

The North had more paper mills, printing presses, newspapers, and reporters than the South, as well as a larger, more literate population.

Both Union and Confederate spies relied on papers from enemy cities for information on the size and location of troops. The agents would scan for helpful details and listen to the reactions of people in the streets to gain an impression of public morale.

Dᴜʀɪɴɢ ᴛʜᴇ 1860s, television and radio had not been invented. "News" traveled most rapidly in the form of rumors passed from one person to the next; however, the accuracy was suspect at best. The most dependable source of information on battles, deaths, troop activities, and other details of the war was the newspaper.

News reporters accompanied front-line troops and wrote detailed, often poetic accounts of battle, sending handwritten reports via messenger or telegraph back to their editors. For a salary of twenty-five dollars a week, journalists dodged bullets and pushed themselves to beat rival reporters for the next day's headlines.

Peter W. Alexander, a reporter for the *Charleston Courier*, described the daily life of a field reporter as "not the most convenient or agreeable task." "Writing on a march . . . there are few times or places [to] set himself consistently down to the work," he wrote. "A man is forced to [use] the crumbling end of a lead pencil, with a . . . fence rail for his writing desk, . . . in sunshine and storm, jerking out his thoughts whenever he can get a chance."

In the early years of the war, the Pony Express carried correspondents'

"What a day! I feel like one who has been out in a high wind, and cannot get my breath. The newsboys are still shouting with their extras, 'Battle of Bull's Run! List of the killed! Battle of Manassas! List of the wounded!'"

Resident of New Orleans, June 1861

In addition to the fearless reporters who wrote about the war, some newspapers paid illustrators to sketch scenes. Though the accuracy of their drawings was sometimes questionable, the artists gave people at home a way to picture the scenes of battle and the condition of the troops, as well as giving "faces" to the leaders' names they heard. By war's end, several young, talented artists had gained fame for their detailed depictions, especially in the popular Leslie's Illustrated and Harper's Weekly.

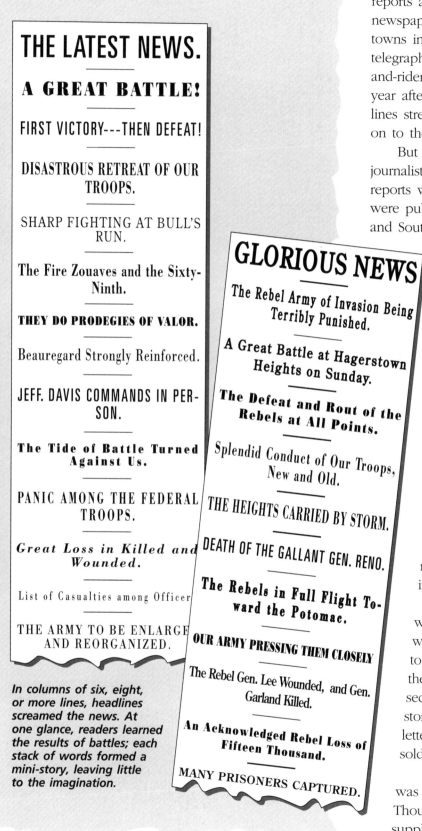

In columns of six, eight, or more lines, headlines screamed the news. At one glance, readers learned the results of battles; each stack of words formed a mini-story, leaving little to the imagination.

reports and copies of eastern newspapers hundreds of miles to towns in the West, though the telegraph soon outdated the horse-and-rider relays. Little more than a year after the war started, telegraph lines stretched west to Missouri and on to the booming state of California.

But from Maine to Georgia, journalists' accounts—and reprints of reports written by military leaders—were published throughout the North and South. When General William Tecumseh Sherman's troops captured Atlanta, Georgia, on September 2, 1864, within just a day or two, readers in New York had detailed stories of the northern occupation and terrible destruction. To satisfy the public's craving for the latest news, the *New York Herald* was reported to have spent half a million dollars—an unbelievably extravagant sum—in telegraph fees, writers' expenses, and transportation costs, to rush reports from the war front to its offices in New York.

At small-town papers, which were usually published weekly, editors couldn't afford to pay correspondents. Instead, they filled their papers with second-hand news, reprints of stories from larger papers, or letters mailed in from local soldiers.

For southern newspapers, it was a struggle to stay in business. Though news was plentiful, supplies of everything from bullets

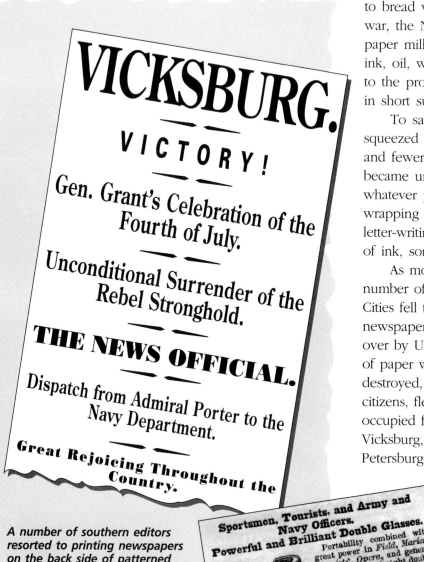

VICKSBURG.

VICTORY!

Gen. Grant's Celebration of the Fourth of July.

Unconditional Surrender of the Rebel Stronghold.

THE NEWS OFFICIAL.

Dispatch from Admiral Porter to the Navy Department.

Great Rejoicing Throughout the Country.

A number of southern editors resorted to printing newspapers on the back side of patterned wallpaper, like the Daily Citizen in Vicksburg, Mississippi, pictured here. The determined staff of the Daily Citizen continued to print an issue even while the city was under constant bombardment by General Grant's army. When the city finally fell, Union troops took over the office and immediately published a celebratory July 4 edition.

Meanwhile, northern publishers faced few such limitations. They churned out issues filled with news reports, serialized stories, and a wealth of advertisements.

to bread were dwindling. Before the war, the North had twenty times more paper mills than the South. And now, ink, oil, wood, and paper—all essential to the production of newspapers—were in short supply.

To save paper, publishers squeezed stories onto smaller sheets and fewer pages. When newsprint became unavailable, publishers gathered whatever paper they could find: brown wrapping paper, thin tissue paper, and letter-writing paper. When they ran out of ink, some even used shoe polish.

As months turned into years, the number of southern papers diminished. Cities fell to northern troops, and the newspapers shut down or were taken over by Union supporters. Warehouses of paper were burned, printing presses destroyed, and editors, like most citizens, fled for safety as Union troops occupied first New Orleans, then Vicksburg, Atlanta, Richmond, and Petersburg. By the time General Lee surrendered to General Grant in April 1865, only about twenty southern newspapers remained. ☆

PHOTOGRAPHING THE WAR

This solemn-looking Confederate soldier undoubtedly maintained his stoic look not only to avoid blurring the picture but also to appear tough. He's wearing two bowie knives and a pistol and holds a saber bayonet and a musket—common weapons for a posed picture, but far more than most soldiers carried into battle.

Cameras used during the Civil War were large and supported by tripods. This unidentified photographer, posing here during a stop in Tennessee, worked with Union photographer George N. Barnard throughout the South. Portraits of photographers were unusual, since most traveled alone and did not take pictures of themselves.

THE CIVIL WAR WAS the first major war in our nation's history in which photography existed. Photographs offered a visual record of the conflict—of the soldiers, the events, and, to a lesser degree, the actual battles. When the war began in 1861, photography had been in existence for only twenty-two years, but it was becoming very popular throughout the country. As young men by the thousands enlisted for military service, they also rushed to the local photography studio to have their portrait taken.

Many of the people photographed had never seen a camera before, so the experience was new and somewhat mysterious to them. Nearly all the portraits feature stiff or posed expressions; rarely does anyone have a smile.

Many of the new soldiers wanted to appear serious for the camera as they headed off to war, but the main reason people looked so unnatural was that exposure times were much longer than today. Now, snapshots can be taken in a fraction of a second, but early photography required subjects to sit perfectly still for as long as ten seconds. People often had their heads placed in metal clamps hidden behind them so they would hold steady enough to avoid blurring the image.

The photographic developing processes used during the Civil War also

In Camp near Huntsville, Alabama
Thursday, January 26th, 1865

My Dear Wife,

I believe I wrote you from Indianapolis that I had made the acquaintance of one William Potter from Lagrange County, Indiana. He is in Company C and is a very fine man I think. Many of our comrades think we look very much alike and we call ourselves cousins. He has his wife's likeness with him. She looks tolerable well, but I am anxious to show him mine. I hope you have sent it so I will get it in the next mail. He and I intended to have our photographs taken together and send to our respective wives and I think we will yet, before we come home. Then you can see for yourself whether there is a family resemblance. He says if we get home he shall visit us with his wife, and so get acquainted all around. I hope he will....

Your Husband, John W. Potter

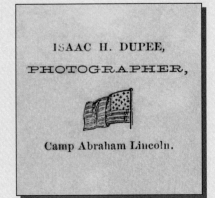

ISAAC H. DUPEE,

PHOTOGRAPHER,

Camp Abraham Lincoln.

To meet the increasing demand for portraits, photographers opened for business in towns and army camps, and even in traveling wagons. Here, Isaac Dupee—and French & Sawyer's and S. J. Atkinson, at right—advertise their services.

Many soldiers posed with friends when they enlisted, or for camp portraits taken by traveling photographers. These two unidentified soldiers shared a similar appearance; but, even more importantly, they shared a bond of friendship that helped sustain them during the long months of tedious days and fierce battles.

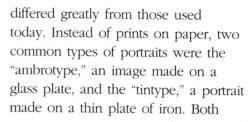

Few photographs of soldiers and sailors depicting harbors, woods, or other outdoor scenes were actually taken outside the studio. To give the illusion of an outdoor shot, many photographers used elaborately painted backdrops, such as this one portraying a fictitious harbor.

differed greatly from those used today. Instead of prints on paper, two common types of portraits were the "ambrotype," an image made on a glass plate, and the "tintype," a portrait made on a thin plate of iron. Both ambrotypes and tintypes were displayed under glass in ornate brass frames and secured in folding cases.

In response to requests from loved ones at home, soldiers paid about one dollar each for portraits—or "likenesses"— taken by traveling photographers, who set up temporary studios in tents pitched near army camps. The ambrotypes and tintypes they took were one-of-a-kind photographs. The camera did not produce a negative from which additional copies could be made. Therefore, every ambrotype or tintype is a unique historical record. Unfortunately, most of these traveling photographers did not identify their work in any way, so today we have virtually no record of the field photographers who played such an important role in documenting the war.

Another popular form of photography was the carte de visite portrait. (Carte de visite is French for "visiting card.") Unlike ambrotypes and tintypes, these portraits were printed from glass negatives and mounted on small paper cards. For three to five dollars, a soldier could purchase a dozen of them to send home to his family and friends.

Because it took more time to

PHOTOGRAPHER AND SOLDIER

Before the war began, an Englishman named Abraham Cottrell moved to Lansing, Michigan, and opened a photography studio. In August 1861, four months after the bombing of Fort Sumter, the thirty-five-year-old Cottrell left his shop and enlisted as a first lieutenant in Company E, "The Elder Zouaves," of the Eighth Michigan Volunteers. While he was away, Cottrell's partner, Phillip Englehart, continued to run the business.

Cottrell served during several fights and skirmishes, including the capture of Port Royal, South Carolina. In April 1862, the photographer-turned-soldier broke his shoulder when his horse fell on him. After making a partial recovery, he returned to service and fought at Secessionville, South Carolina, where he was injured again and taken as a prisoner of war. After four months in Confederate prisons, Cottrell was exchanged and sent north.

Still suffering from his ill-healed shoulder, he was discharged in 1863; his commander recognized him as "a True soldier and a Brave man."

During the next two years, Cottrell continued to serve the Union, first in the Invalid Corps and later as a trainer of new recruits. Cottrell returned to his business while the war continued, but did little photography.

He was finally discharged in September 1865. His war injuries left him in poor health and he had trouble handling the heavy cameras and equipment; but he continued as a photographer for many years.

Cottrell lived in Michigan until his death in 1901 at the age of seventy-five.

This army building is probably in Elmira, New York, where Cottrell served during the war after being released by the Confederate Army. The tintype belonged to Cottrell, and while it is possible that he is one of the men pictured, as in many Civil War photographs, there is no means of verifying the exact identities of the people.

Photographers such as Abraham Cottrell, who had permanent studios, printed their names on the back of cartes de visite to identify their work and attract new customers.

create the glass negative, make the prints, and mount them on cards, carte de visite portraits were usually taken by photographers who had permanent studios in towns and cities rather than by traveling photographers.

More than 125 years ago, the invention and widespread use of photography gave Union and Confederate soldiers the chance to document their experiences in a vivid new way. Thousands of the soldiers pictured never returned from the war to see their friends and families again.

Today, these images provide more than a snapshot view of America going to war: They offer a lasting look at the real people—old and young, Northerner and Southerner—who gave so much for what they believed. ☆

BATTLING BOREDOM

Battle - Hymn
of
The Republic.

Mine eyes have seen the glory of the
coming of the Lord:
He is trampling out the vintage where the
grapes of wrath are stored;
He hath loosed the fateful lightning of his
terrible swift sword:
His truth is marching on.

I have seen Him in the watch-fires of
an hundred circling camps;
They have builded Him an altar in the
evening dews and damps;
I can read H...

Hi...

In the autumn of 1861, after watching a grand review of the troops in Washington, D.C., Julia Ward Howe woke in the middle of the night and scribbled the lyrics to "The Battle Hymn of the Republic." Atlantic Monthly magazine published the poem in February 1862, paying Howe four dollars. Sung to the popular tune of "John Brown's Body," her emotionally stirring, patriotic words became an immediate favorite in Union camps.

Publishers took advantage of the fervor for wartime songs, producing sheet music and song books with old favorites and popular new songs. "Just Before the Battle, Mother," pictured here, became popular with both Union and Confederate troops; hundreds of other new songs never caught on in popularity.

Fort Monroe, outside Norfolk, Virginia, never changed hands during the war. Union troops stationed there had time to assemble a well-equipped and handsomely dressed band.

THE MEN AND BOYS WHO served during the war worked harder than ever before in their lives. They marched hundreds of miles, suffered constant illness, and endured bloody battles. It was a violent and exhausting experience, yet often, a boring one.

Whether they were trying to stay awake during late-night sentry duty, digging trenches, or recuperating in a hospital, soldiers had hours, days, and even months with little to occupy their time.

One of the soldiers' best weapons against boredom was music. They played fiddles, harmonicas, and banjos, and sung sentimental ballads while gathered around the campfire. They whistled favorite tunes as they dug latrines or cleaned their weapons. On the march, the men sang rhythmic battle hymns to lift their spirits and keep their minds off weary legs.

Southern troops favored "The Bonnie Blue Flag," "Home Sweet Home," and "Dixie," while Union soldiers sang "Rally Round the Flag," "John Brown's Body," and "Tenting on the Old Campground." Many new songs were written during the war, but soldiers often preferred such old

"We are coming, Father Abraham,
Three hundred thousand more,
From Mississippi's winding stream
And from New England's shore;
We leave our plows and workshops,
Our wives and children dear,
With hearts too full for utterance,
With but a silent tear;
We dare not look behind us,
But steadfastly before.
We are coming, Father Abraham,
Three hundred thousand more!"

In 1862, the song "We Are Coming, Father Abraham" swept Union camps. Inspired by President Lincoln's call for an additional three hundred thousand volunteers in July of that year, the song was certainly more popular than the draft laws that followed.

Drummer boys were the pride of their company. Too young to enlist, they found a way to serve, marching (and often falling) with their men.

Midway through the war, with rumpled uniforms and dented saber scabbards, these infantry officers pause in the field to smoke their pipes and enjoy a glass of wine.

A Harper's Weekly correspondent made this sketch of soldiers from the Army of the Potomac dancing in camp "after evening parade," in the fall of 1861.

favorites as "Yankee Doodle Dandy," "Shoo Fly Shoo," and "Pop Goes the Weasel." Their well-known lyrics, which everyone could sing, reminded soldiers of home. Almost every camp, Confederate or Union, had an informal "homemade" band composed of every size and shape of instrument the men could manage to carry from home. Larger camps assembled formal music and theatrical groups that performed for the general public as well as for military audiences. In a letter to his fiancée in Illinois, one Union soldier described such an event: "There is to be a large ball . . . on the evening of the 16th. I think some of attending. I have no doubt but that it

"Yesterday, being St. Patrick's Day, was celebrated in the 2d Corps by the annual races which are regularly gotten up by the Irish brigade.... There was ... a great deal of sport and fun. The betting also was lively.... Horse racing is prohibited ... and it is only on special occasions, like St. Patrick's Day, that there is any running."

Hazard Stevens, Sixth Corps Staff
March 18, 1865, outside Petersburg, Virginia

While soldiers drill in the foreground, members of the Forty-eighth New York Infantry play a game of baseball at Fort Pulaski, Georgia, in a rare early photograph of "America's game." The popularity of baseball spread rapidly during the Civil War.

Members of the 114th Pennsylvania Infantry relax with a game of cards. The table and chairs, and other camp supplies, would likely be left behind or end up as firewood when the troops relocated.

will be a very elegant affair. Oh, how I wish you were here to go with me! . . . A great many ladies from Washington, Philadelphia, and Baltimore are expected to be there. . . . Still my thoughts would wander to the dear girl . . . on whom my affections are already placed."

In addition to music, there were numerous other diversions in camp. Men passed the time playing checkers, chess, and countless games of cards. One soldier wrote to his mother, "Everything has again quieted down to the old monotony of winter quarters. . . . I have played a number of games of chess lately. . . . The surgeon in chief and I have three or four games every evening. I have not much trouble in beating him."

During mild weather, foot races, wrestling, and even baseball were popular. For those lucky enough to be camped near water, swimming and fishing could fill free time. In the evening, the men read magazines and books, talked with friends, and wrote letters. Some took up carving as a hobby, making poker chips, whistles, and small figurines out of wood and animal bone.

Many men tried to appear tougher and more hardened by the war than they were, posing with weapons, whiskey, and cigars.

People crowded wartime fund-raising exhibitions and fairs in cities throughout the North and South. Though the events were organized with the goal of raising money for the care of soldiers, people flocked to them to enjoy song and dance performances, picture galleries, auctions, fashion shows, and banquets.

Here, people stroll through an exhibition hall at the New York Metropolitan Fair in April 1864.

New York City's Central Park formally opened in 1864, and on winter weekends it bustled with ice skaters. Even at the height of the war, northern cities continued to expand and improve.

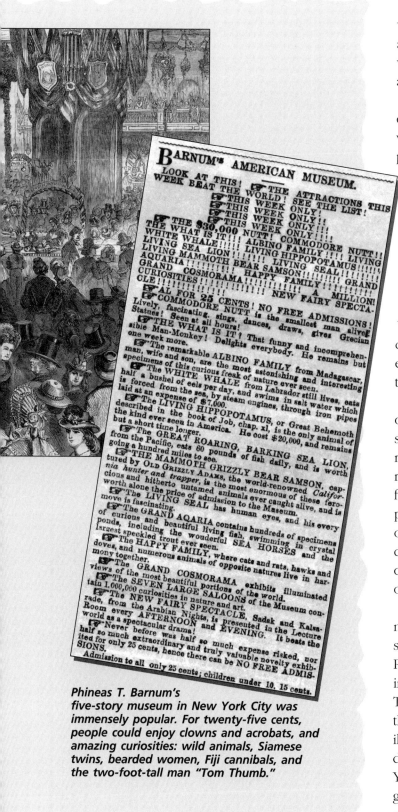

Phineas T. Barnum's five-story museum in New York City was immensely popular. For twenty-five cents, people could enjoy clowns and acrobats, and amazing curiosities: wild animals, Siamese twins, bearded women, Fiji cannibals, and the two-foot-tall man "Tom Thumb."

For people on the home front, worried about their loved ones far away in the army, finding pleasurable ways to pass the time was often just as difficult as for the soldiers.

Ironically, the first major entertainment of the war was the war itself. People attended speeches, parades, and rallies to express their patriotism and political views, as well as to see and be seen socially. When Union and Confederate troops clashed in the first major battle of the war on July 21, 1861, at Bull Run (Manassas, as the Confederates called it), the fighting took place in Virginia dangerously close to Washington, D.C. A number of civilians—women in fancy dresses, and even congressmen—gathered on hilltops to watch as if it were a sporting event.

At first the spectators saw clouds of smoke caused by thousands of rifle shots, and they cheered results they received via telegraph. But chaos resulted when the fighting turned in favor of the South. Union soldiers panicked and fled, overtaking civilians on the road. The battle resulted in disastrous losses for Union troops and quickly destroyed the romantic view of the war held by so many people.

As the war dragged on for months, and then years, civilian life still maintained a level of normalcy. People went ice skating and sledding in winter and swimming in summer. They attended plays and operas, read the latest popular books, and browsed illustrated newspapers. With spirits dampened by war from Atlanta to New York, people sought entertainment that gave them a fleeting escape from the nation's troubles and instilled hope for a renewed peace. ☆

MARCHING HOME

On April 9, 1865, General Lee met General Grant in the parlor of a house at Appomattox Courthouse, where Lee signed the truce that ended the war. In the following weeks, the South's remaining armies surrendered.

> When Johnny comes marching home again,
> Hurrah! Hurrah!
> We'll give him a hearty welcome then,
> Hurrah! Hurrah!
> The men will cheer, the boys will shout,
> The ladies they will all turn out,
> And we'll all feel gay
> When Johnny comes marching home.

Written by Patrick S. Gilmore, "When Johnny Comes Marching Home" was a favorite song among Union soldiers heading home in spring 1865.

On May 23 and 24, 1865, two hundred thousand Union soldiers marched in a Grand Review up Pennsylvania Avenue in Washington, D.C. By 1866, the Union Army had decreased in size from more than one million soldiers to just eighty thousand men. For Confederates, the trip home was more difficult. Traveling on foot for hundreds of miles, they straggled south. Many found their homes—and lives—in shambles.

Six Miles East of Appomattox Court House, Va.
April 10th, 1865

Dear Mother,
There is no longer an Army of Northern Virginia. Lee surrendered the remainder of his army yesterday afternoon, about 20,000 men, I believe. The last hope of the Rebellion is extinguished. . . . Thus in a campaign of 7 days, the rebel army, which has held us in check for four years, was annihilated. . . . I hope to be home for good in a few months now. No more drilling. No more going under artillery and musketry fire, and shouting yourself hoarse. . . . Our fights are over.

Your affectionate son,
Hazard Stevens

On Sunday morning, April 2, 1865, Jefferson Davis was in church in Richmond, Virginia, when he received the inevitable news: Union troops were advancing on the South's capital. It was the beginning of the end for the Confederacy.

As rebel soldiers evacuated Richmond, they burned valuable supplies to keep them from falling into Yankee hands. The next day, President Lincoln and his son Tad visited the still-burning city. Gathered in the streets, Union soldiers and former slaves greeted Lincoln ecstatically. At the same time that Davis was fleeing south, Lincoln entered the Confederate president's office and sat in the very chair from which Davis had directed the now-crumbling Confederacy.

The news of the fall of Richmond was devastating to General Lee's starving and despondent army. Clothed in rags, his men struggled to continue the fight. But on April 9, as Union Major Hazard Stevens, who was positioned nearby, described, "Lee found [Union General] Sheridan posted at Appomattox Court House in force. . . . He had no alternative but to surrender or have his army crushed between our columns." Rather than sacrifice his men, Lee recognized that the fight was over. The Union had won.

As news spread through the troops, the reaction on both sides was immediate and intense. "You can't imagine what a time we had last night,

OUR GREAT LOSS

Death of President Lincoln.

The Songs of Victory Drowned in Sorrow.

CLOSING SCENES OF A NOBLE LIFE.

The Great Sorrow of an Afflicted Nation.

Party Differences Forgotten in Public Grief.

Vice-President Johnson Inaugurated as Chief Executive.

MR. SEWARD WILL RECOVER.

John Wilkes Booth Believed to be the Assassin.

Church bells tolled as thousands of people lined the streets of Washington, D.C., to view the slow, grim spectacle of Lincoln's funeral parade. The president's body was carried to the Capitol, where he lay in state the next day.

The government offered large rewards for information leading to the capture of Lincoln's assassin, John Wilkes Booth. Less than two weeks after the president's death, Federal troops trapped Booth in a Virginia barn where he was shot and killed.

such cheering I never heard," wrote Stevens. "My new horse almost threw me. She was very much frightened. All the artillery fired salutes. Such a roar of guns, more than a great battle. Everybody was mad with joy."

And, as hard as it was for the southern troops to give up their cause, many felt relief that finally they could go home.

After four long years, the country was again one.

Just as Americans turned to the task of reuniting the country, a bolt of lightning struck: On April 14, President Lincoln was assassinated. He had been attending a play at Ford's Theater in Washington, D.C., when a man named John Wilkes Booth slipped into the balcony box behind the president and shot him in the head. The assassin jumped to the stage twelve feet below, breaking his left shinbone, and fled through the stage door, where a waiting horse carried him off. By morning, Lincoln had died, and Andrew Johnson, his vice president, suddenly had charge of a country devastated by war and in shock at the loss of Lincoln.

A funeral was held in the capital city, where the streets were draped in black. A train carrying Lincoln's body set off for his final resting place in Illinois. At stop after stop along the sixteen-hundred-mile path, mourners lined up to view the coffin of the fallen hero.

Lincoln had worked tirelessly to reunite the states but died before he could see his vision become reality. Just a month earlier, in his second Inaugural Address, he had spoken with emotion and urgency of rebuilding the

The Soldier's grave.

New cemeteries dotted the countryside, from large plots of land with thousands of evenly spaced headstones to small sites marked with just a few roughly hewn crosses or low mounds of dirt.

In November 1863, when President Lincoln delivered his now-famous Gettysburg Address at the dedication of the new cemetery in Pennsylvania, he summed up the grief and frustration of losing so many men. "We here highly resolve," he said, "that these dead shall not have died in vain—that this nation, under God, shall have a new birth of freedom—and that government of the people, by the people, for the people, shall not perish from the earth."

For generations, the gravesites have served as a grim reminder of the fierce battles Americans waged against one another during the War Between the States.

nation: "With malice toward none; with charity for all . . . let us strive on . . . to bind up the nation's wounds, to care for him who shall have borne the battle, and for his widow, and his orphan." Let us do all, Lincoln declared, "to achieve and cherish a just and lasting peace among ourselves, and with all nations."

The Civil War had cost 620,000 soldiers their lives—360,000 Federals and 260,000 Confederates. Hundreds of thousands more were wounded, and the lives of millions of people were changed forever.

In the South, people struggled to find their way in a world so different than before—the Confederacy was broken, their slaves were free, and their cities and plantations lay in ruins. It would take decades to recover.

In the North, where few battles had been fought, there was far less physical destruction and recovery came quickly. An influx of immigrants brought new energy and hope with them. Northern industry was booming, and people looked with optimism to the West, where the government would give land to anyone willing to make a five-year commitment to clearing and farming it.

The casualties of war were far-reaching: For every soldier who died, there were many more who were crippled for life.

For black Americans, who had finally won freedom from slavery, the coming years brought a new fight—to attain equal status in a country that still viewed them as second-class citizens.

And so, with the war behind them, Americans—north and south—turned to the new challenges of reuniting, rebuilding, and expanding as a nation. ☆

89

GLOSSARY

abolitionist   a person who worked to end slavery in the United States

ambrotype   an early type of photograph in which the image was printed on a glass plate and held in a brass frame

artillery   a branch of the armed forces that operates large mounted guns, too heavy to carry; also, the guns themselves

bayonet   a long, narrow-bladed knife designed to fit on the end of a rifle barrel and to be used in hand-to-hand combat

blockade   to prevent the entry and exit of ships from a harbor

carte de visite   an early type of photograph in which the image was printed from a glass negative onto a paper card

casualty   a soldier, who, during a battle, is killed, wounded, captured, or missing in action

cavalry   a branch of the army trained to fight on horseback

Confederate States of America   the alliance of eleven southern states that withdrew from the United States in 1860 and 1861: Alabama, Arkansas, Florida, Georgia, Louisiana, Mississippi, North Carolina, South Carolina, Tennessee, Texas, and Virginia. Also referred to as the Confederacy.

contraband   a slave who escaped to or was brought into Union lines

Democrat   a member of the political party that supported slavery and believed states should control their own affairs without interference from the national government

desert to leave the armed forces without permission and with no intention of returning

draft the government's selection of citizens for a required period of military service

dysentery a painful, and sometimes fatal, disorder of the intestines, characterized by severe diarrhea

emancipate to free from slavery

Emancipation Proclamation an act issued by President Lincoln in 1862 that freed all slaves in the rebel states

enlist to join the armed services

Federal having to do with the union of states that recognized the authority of the United States government based in Washington, D.C.

infantry a branch of the army made up of units trained to fight on foot

malaria a serious disease causing high fevers and chills, often spread by the bite of an infected mosquito

musket a long-barreled gun carried by infantry and fired from the shoulder

muster to call together a group of soldiers; to enlist someone in, or discharge someone from, military service

ordnance military weapons, ammunition, and equipment

pleurisy the inflammation of the sacs surrounding the lungs, which makes breathing and coughing extremely painful

provisions necessary supplies, especially food

rebel another term for a Confederate soldier or a civilian supporter of the Confederacy

recruit to persuade a person to join the armed services; a person who enlists in the armed services

scurvy a disease caused by lack of vitamin C, marked by soft and bleeding gums, bleeding under the skin, and extreme weakness

secession the withdrawal from membership in an organization or group

sentry a guard who prevents the passage of unauthorized persons

smallpox a highly infectious, and often fatal, disease, marked by a high fever and blistering spots on the skin

states' rights   the ability of individual states to control their own affairs without interference from the government in Washington, D.C.

tintype   an early type of photograph in which the image was printed on a thin plate of iron held in a brass frame

typhoid   a serious disease, often caused by ingesting contaminated food or water; the symptoms are a high fever, spots on the skin, coughing, and heavy intestinal bleeding

Union   another name for the United States of America, used especially during the Civil War

Yankee   another name for a Northerner

SELECTED BIBLIOGRAPHY

Abbot, Willis J. *Battle Fields and Camp Fires: A Narrative of the Principal Military Operations of the Civil War.* New York: Dodd, Mead & Company, 1890.

Anderson, J. Cutler. *The South Reports the Civil War.* Princeton, N.J.: Princeton University Press, 1970.

Beebe, Angie C. *The Boys in Blue: An Original Collection of War Poems and War Songs of the American Civil War.* Red Wing, Minn.: The Argus Press, 1903.

Blackford, Charles Minor III, ed. *Letters from Lee's Army, or, Memoirs of Life In and Out of the Army in Virginia During the War Between the States.* New York: Charles Scribner's Sons, 1947.

Brown, Leonard. *American Patriotism; or Memoirs of "Common Men."* Des Moines: Redhead and Wellslager, 1869.

Burton, E. P. *Diary of E. P. Burton: Surgeon 7th Reg. Ill. 3rd Brig. 2nd Div. 16 A.C.* Des Moines: The Historical Records Survey, 1939.

Channing, Stephen A., ed. *The Confederate Ordeal: The Southern Home Front.* (Time-Life American Civil War Series). Alexandria, Va.: Time-Life Books, 1984.

Chesnut, Mary. *A Diary from Dixie.* Cambridge: Harvard University Press, 1980.

Davis, Keith. *George N. Barnard: Photographer of Sherman's Campaign.* Kansas City: Hallmark Cards, 1990.

Davis, William C. *Rebels & Yankees: The Fighting Men of the Civil War.* New York: Gallery Books, 1989.

Doubleday, Abner. *Reminiscences of Forts Sumter and Moultrie in 1860–'61.* Fort Sumter National Monument Library, 1876. Reprint. Spartanburg, S.C.: The Reprint Company, 1976.

Famous Adventures and Prison Escapes of the Civil War. New York: The Century Company, 1913.

Freeman, Douglas Southall, ed. *A Calendar of Confederate Papers.* Richmond, Va.: The Confederate Museum, 1908.

Goss, Warren Lee. *The Soldier's Story of His Captivity at Andersonville, Belle Isle and Other Rebel Prisons.* Boston: Lee & Shepard, 1866.

Jackson, Donald Dale, ed. *Twenty Million Yankees: The Northern Home Front.* (Time-Life American Civil War Series). Alexandria, Va.: Time-Life Books, 1985.

Karolevitz, Robert F. *From Quill to Computer: The Story of America's Community Newspapers.* National Newspaper Foundation, 1985.

Kieffer, Harry M. *The Recollections of a Drummer Boy.* Boston: Houghton Mifflin, 1881.

Livermore, Mary A. *My Story of the War: A Woman's Narrative.* Hartford, Conn.: A. D. Worthington & Company, 1889.

Logan, Mrs. John A. *Reminiscences of a Soldier's Wife.* New York: Charles Scribner's Sons, 1913.

McPherson, James M. *Battle Cry of Freedom: The Civil War Era.* New York: Ballantine Books, 1988.

Moore, Frank. *Women of the War; Their Heroism and Self-sacrifice.* Hartford, Conn.: S. S. Scranton & Company, 1867.

Robertson, James I., ed. *Tenting Tonight: The Soldier's Life.* (Time-Life American Civil War Series). Alexandria, Va.: Time-Life Books, 1984.

Rogers, Rev. J. B. *War Pictures: Pictures and Observations of a Chaplain in the U.S. Army.* Chicago: Church & Goodman, 1863.

Roth, David E. *The Illustrated History of the Civil War, 1861–1865.* New York: Smithmark, 1992.

Silber, Irwin. *Soldier Songs and Home-front Ballads of the Civil War.* New York: Oak Publications, 1964.

Sutherland, Daniel E. *The Expansion of Everyday Life: 1860–1876.* New York: Harper & Row, 1989.

Wiley, Bell Irvin. *The Life of Billy Yank: The Common Soldier of the Union.* Garden City, N.Y.: Doubleday, 1971.

———. *The Life of Johnny Reb: The Common Soldier of the Confederacy.* New York: The Bobs-Merrill Company, 1943.

Wright, D. Giraud. *A Southern Girl in '61: The War-Time Memories of a Confederate Senator's Daughter.* New York: Doubleday, Page & Company, 1905.

PICTURE CREDITS

The photographs and illustrations in this book are from the following sources. The images are public domain or are used with the source's permission.

Images are listed by single page or two-page spreads in this order: left-hand page, top to bottom; right-hand page, top to bottom.

Abbreviations

CPL	Chicago Public Library, Special Collections Department
Leib	Leib Image Archives, York, Pa.
LOC	Library of Congress, Washington, D.C.
Wilcox	Collection of Kean Wilcox, Pullman, Wash.